Rebound

Rebound

Rising from failure back to purpose and destiny

William Baldwin

XULON ELITE

Xulon Press Elite
2301 Lucien Way #415
Maitland, FL 32751
407.339.4217
www.xulonpress.com

Edited by Xulon Press.

Printed in the United States of America.

ISBN-13: 9781545641835

Dedication

To

The City of Albemarle

G rowing up, you were an ordinary landmark, a mere blip on my way to the beach. Years later, I came to live with you, and you adopted me as part of your family. I rose and fell, then by God's grace grappled my way back to stand amongst you once again. I dedicate this book to my city—my people.

Chapters

Acknowledgments

My precious wife, Karen, reflects the nature of God in that she, better than anyone else on the planet, knows my frame, that I am but mere dust. She is my Proverbs 31 lady, "a good wife worth more than precious gems." Together, we have trudged up mountains, through valleys and across the leveled plains of life on our way to our destiny. Our journey has not been an easy one, but she has walked with me every step of the way. My Karen, I love you.

Eddie and Betty Gouldman, my spiritual father and mother, recognized God's grace on me early on after I surrendered my life to Jesus. When I was a young believer, they imparted to me a passion for the Presence of God. One day heaven will unveil how profoundly Eddie and Betty impacted the lives of so many people. The effects of their lives upon a young preacher continues as I approach my golden years of ministry and life.

My church family, Harvest Church, loves me in spite of myself. They know me to be like a six-stringed guitar with only three strings. The older I get, the more I harp on (literally) a few subjects I consider essential—at least, essential to me. At this juncture in our history, the Holy Spirit is playing a distinct sound through us. And while we may not be a full-stringed instrument, we pluck the heck out of the ones we have. I love you all.

Kimberly Shumate was my writing agent who pitched my first book, He Restores, to countless publishers. Her relentless praise for that book written to leaders made me feel as though I was a better writer than I am. Eight years ago she insisted I write a similar book to the average person. Finally, here it is. Thanks, Kimberly, for planting that seed.

Finally, I am indebted to countless others, through their books, teaching and friendship. In one of Leonard Ravenhill's writings, he admits to being like "a bee gathering from many flowers." I understand. Within these pages, there are, without doubt, thoughts, ideas and revelations not original with me. I've tried to give credit to those sources I remember. If I did not, join me in providing supreme recognition to the One to whom all truth originates.

Foreword

The prefix "re" is found over 400 times in the Bible in words such as, remember, return, renew, revive and restore. In his own unique and down-to-earth style, Bill Baldwin is exemplary, taking rich and redemptive words, and providing us with a truth that is tangible, real and genuine.

Baldwin's authenticity and transparency about his own journey is a breath of fresh air in a time when many are marginalized for their failures. I have had the privilege of knowing Bill for over 20 years, and I can attest to the fact that he is not a mere theorist when it comes to the challenging call to rebound from failure to fulfill his purpose and destiny.

Rebound articulates with clarity the noble responsibility we have as humans to echo someone else's pain. In Jesus, God became flesh so He could live empathically through us. The purpose of the incarnation was not merely to save us from our sin but to save us from ourselves. Our instinct is to insulate and isolate to protect ourselves from potential rejection or incrimination by association. Bill calls those who have failed, as well as the spectators of their fall out of the shadows to acknowledge God's restorative nature.

You hold in your hands a redemptive story as well as a field manual for all of us who are learning to walk through our own brokenness and embrace the brokenness of the human family. You will be glad you took the time to read this timely work from a true purveyor of hope.

Dr. Randall Worley, Author of Brush Strokes of Grace
and Wandering and Wondering

Words of Praise For Rebound...

Here's an honest and heartfelt story that keeps you reading!

This book offers hope to those who have no hope or believe they are finished and sidelined forever. Bill's words remind us of the grace of the Cross and what Jesus wants to do in our lives because He loves us so very much. Anyone who feels they're too broken for God to restore, needs to read *Rebound*. Ministry leaders should have this resource available to share with those who need the hope of Jesus Christ. This book will change your life!

Gina Russell, Executive Director,
Pregnancy Resource Center

You can't change what's happened, but you can change what happens next. What kind of mess have you made in your life? How are you feeling about yourself in light of the wreckage behind you? What defines you? What have you lost in life? What will you do with it? Better yet, what will God do with it? It's not so much what we have done to our lives as much as what God will do with it this point forward.

William Baldwin's work, *Rebound: Rising from Failure Back to Purpose and Destiny* expertly guides you through the journey from where you are to where God has purposed you to be. He doesn't claim the journey will be easy, but his experience will undoubtedly help you follow the heart of God toward your own purpose and destiny God ordained for you.

The apostle John, the disciple whom Jesus loved, wrote, "I remind you, my dear children, your sins are forgiven in Jesus name" (1 John 2:12, The Message). With the help of the book you hold in your hand you can fully realize God's plan for your life. Get back in the game! Regardless of your past, you can finish well.

Dr. Don Bartley, LMFT

William Baldwin's first book "He Restores" was a God send to me during a very tough time in my life. It was integral to my restoration process after a hard fall. I was thrilled to read his latest book, *Rebound*. This book is a must-read for anyone who feels they have failed, both with what the world may expect of us and what we expect of ourselves. These chapters reach into the depths of your soul. I highly recommend meditating on its entirety and apply the truth found throughout these pages in your daily life.

Tracy L Meyer, Worship Leader

Are you in a season of failure? Do you know someone sidelined because of failure? Bill charts a course to help you grow from failure and get back into the parade of life.

All have fallen short of his purpose and all are invited to his table to recover from their failure. I've encouraged students and families many times to "learn the lesson" and move one step at the time into God's plan and destiny that still awaits them. The apostle Paul said we are saved by grace through faith not by works, but rather for good works. In advance, God planned for us to walk in those good works. That's destiny! There is hope, healing and recovery from failure.

In this excellent book, *Rebound*, let Bill guide and mentor you forward toward the hope and future God has for you.

John Steigerwald, Executive Director of
North Carolina Boys Academy (Teen Challenge)

All of us, if we have any conscience at all, are aware that we are guilty. Some of us are guiltier of heinous sins than others. But, we cannot whitewash our own by magnifying the sins of others.

One of the first verses I remember is Romans 3:23-24, "All have sinned and fall short of the glory of God, being justified as a gift by His grace through the redemption which is in Christ Jesus. With that one, I learned, "The wages of sin is death, but the free gift of God is eternal life in Christ Jesus our Lord (Romans 6:23).

We are all in the same boat—fellows in the same ship!

Receiving God's grace sets us free from the fruits of our self-life, and become benefactors of a new creation. "If anyone is in Christ, he is a new creature; the old things passed away; behold, new things have come" (1 Corinthians 5:17).

Rebound is a powerful resource for anyone in this process. Bill's book is the testimony of one who walked out of failure, and passes along to you the benefits of his journey. Admitting he's still processing, he imparts faith and practical revelation as you rebound back to your own purpose and destiny.

Don Atkin, apostolic father/leader

Preface

The day after I finished the final manuscript for this book, I experienced a mysterious vision. It came early in the morning in a cozy room above our garage where I do my reading, writing, meditating and praying. The brief ten-minute encounter was like streaming a video through my mind. After it played out, I knew I had to include this in the book.

I saw what appeared to be a parade moving down a city street. As the procession funneled down the avenue, I became aware that I was not only watching but was also part of it. Colorful floats and lovely beauty queens crept along, while marching bands trumpeted happy tunes. People, whom I assumed were there to watch the celebration, were shoulder-to-shoulder alongside the road.

As the scene played out, I noticed occasional gaps in the convoy of celebrants. As much as fifteen minutes would pass with dead silence. No band, no float, no anything. After the awkward time lapse, the next leg of the parade would round the bend, and the gala continued.

Though it only lasted about ten minutes, these fifteen-minute breaks in the parade didn't logically add up. It's strange how spirit-time doesn't always fit into real-time. Nonetheless, this was how the movie-like vision came to me.

Toward the end I fastened my attention on the people standing alongside the road. The parade, I then realized, was not the center of attention. Instead, we who marched along became focused on the string of people on either side of us. *They* were the point and message of the vision.

Looking closer, I beheld every kind of person one could imagine. I'm not capable of describing the spectacle of humanity. Every race, language, nationality, physical stature, health status, emotional state, spiritual background and condition stood along the streets. A vast diversity of social, economic, spiritual, emotional, mental and physical conditions was represented.

Some wore rags, while others dressed in top-of-the-line, name-brand clothing. The people came decked out in every imaginable style and fashion.

I noticed some of the folks were so weary they were hunched over without strength to even sit up. Others seemed extraordinarily active and happy. Some sat alone, but there were also groups of four and five who appeared to be prosperous families with stable mothers and fathers, sons and daughters.

Many of them focused on honorable things like their children, family, their vocation, caring for others and serving people. All of them, no matter their station in life, were good people with values and a belief in God. The downside was that their focus, whether noble or not, was a substitute for something they had lost because of a dark or painful moment in their history. Every person on the side of the road was running, either physically or mentally, from something or someone in their past.

Abruptly, the vision shifted from merely seeing to *feeling*. I was allowed to *feel* the emotion and pain they all felt, which was quite overwhelming. I sensed addictions to drugs, alcohol, sex and pornography, to name a few. The more "well-to-do" were obsessed with riches, notoriety, power and prosperity.

The prevailing mindset was distrust and fear. All the bystanders kept a cautious distance because most believed that people, especially the church, were judgmental and motivated by self-interest. Of course, this isn't true, but that was their perception because it had been their experience. Cynicism was their mark of "maturity," though they were utterly ignorant of how this attitude affected their personalities.

A haunting shame lingered over everyone along the street. Shame especially targeted women who had experienced abortions, as well as the physicians who had become wealthy performing them. I sensed hopelessness in people with mental disorders such as bipolar, schizophrenia and depression. Self-pity entwined itself so profoundly in each one that I knew it would be a daunting task to confront anyone about their condition.

The scene faded, and an understanding of what I saw became crystal clear.

The people beside the road were there for a reason. Something happened that left them "sidelined." Their history was a landfill of failures, falls and disappointments. People they trusted had either taught them or made them feel that their failure disqualified them from fulfilling what they once believed to be their destiny. They feared to fail again. Others were apprehensive about getting hurt again. And so they surrendered their dreams because they thought the best they could do now was support others, like those of us in the parade, in fulfilling theirs.

Suddenly, I understood the reason for those long, eerie gaps of silence among the marching fray. The blank spaces of nothingness were where the people on the side of the street belonged. No one could fill those gaps but them. Since they thought they no longer could, the enormous spaces of silence remained. If the truth were known, the people on the side of the road wanted to join us, but they would dare not attempt to. Not now. Not again. So we walked along weakened and incomplete by their absence.

And the parade? Why we were nothing less than the "triumphal procession" that Paul wrote about to the Corinthian church (see 2 Corinthians 2:14-15). We are the fragrant family of God, who also happen to be an army incognito. We come armed with an unconventional weaponry of love, joy, mercy and grace. As we release these heavenly warheads, people held hostage to guilt, shame, fear and religion, just to mention a few, are set free. We are on a mission to love people, which has been God's mission since the beginning of time.

I have written to you, the fallen and failed, the bruised and battered. Something sidelined you. You did something, or something happened to you. So you resigned yourself from fulfilling your purposes and dreams. You've tried to be okay with it, but you know you don't belong here. Not on the sidelines. It's just not you, to sit and watch.

I am aware that this volume does not contain all the answers, neither does it speak to every specific need of everyone's fall and failure. I argued with God about this myself. His response to my complaint, as always, was classic and wise and disarming. Against my protest of "not being enough," I think I heard Him say. . .

> *"Remember the Samaritan? The man traveling from Jerusalem to Jericho fell into the hands of robbers and was left lying on the side of the road. A priest and Levite passed by and left him there to die. The Samaritan picked him up and carried him to an inn where the innkeeper nursed him back to health. Your part is to pick them up. Tell them they don't have to live and die on the side of the road. I'll provide innkeepers to do the rest."*

That was good enough for me.

I may not answer all your questions, but this much I know. . .

You're not supposed to live the rest of your life *watching us*, but *walking with us*. There's a void in the family that only you can fill. The priests and Levites may have passed over you, but I've come to tell you, you don't have to stay sidelined. Your spot has been empty and silent for too long. God has reserved your place. He, and we, anxiously await your return.

Chapter One

"Restore!"

The Bible reveals that our champions of faith were murderers, adulterers, prostitutes, liars, cheaters, traitors and thieves. Knowing the frailties and failures of these heroic men and women gives me immeasurable hope and encouragement.

It was a hot, sultry Sunday morning in July. Feathery clouds wisped across a sparkling blue sky with humidity so thick you could slice it. It was one of those Southern mornings that sandwiched you between ribbons of heat rising off the sidewalk and rays raining down from the sun.

I scanned our little congregation and noticed a new face among us. We were a young church plant, only a few months old, meeting outside under a sizeable open-air breezeway at a Christian school. Dressed in a suit and tie, our guest stood out among the casual regulars wearing jeans, shorts and flip-flops. It was impossible for a visitor to hide in our small company of worshippers. Everyone noticed him. Besides being hot and miserable in his Sunday best, he stood out to me for other reasons. I could tell he was familiar with church, but I also sensed his uneasiness with us. His churchy appearance gave me the impression he was a church leader, possibly an elder, deacon or maybe even a pastor. I'm sure it was the suit that was a dead giveaway. But he wore something else that caught my eye. I saw pain. To me it was evident, but it is one of those things you have to experience to notice. A Sunday face and your best suit cannot hide this kind of agony.

As it turned out, I was right. He was a pastor and was, indeed, a wounded soul. Somehow I sensed his anguish was self-inflicted, and I discovered later that I was right about that too.

As I preached, he wept. After the worship service was over, I walked over to greet him. It didn't take long for him to open up to me. He was looking for someone who would listen and understand and, if possible, help him heal. He ended up at our church because someone told him I would receive him. With a quivering voice and eyes full, he cut to the chase.

"I need help. Could you meet me for lunch sometime?"

Over lunch the next day he unfolded his account of wrong choices, a sexual affair and financial scandal that made even me shiver.

THE PROBLEM

Another child of God had fallen, and, in this case, a leader had disqualified himself from his purpose and destiny. Little did he know how much listening to him helped me. While hearing him out, I found myself silently asking God for grace not to waste my own failure-filled story. Like the heroes I'd read about in Scripture, I asked God to use it to help others rebound from their fall. You hold in your hands the overflow of that prayer.

Similar stories are commonplace among people of faith, mostly because people of faith are *people*. We have watched the media capitalize on the juicy failures of prominent people in corporate, political and marketplace circles. Not all shortcomings, however, are the result of immorality or misappropriated money. Some fall out of step with God and their destiny due to emotional or mental distress. These miseries can lead to addictions that create a tangled-up mess in their already troubled lives. We are flawed creatures capable of making choices that reflect just how dysfunctional we really are.

Some years ago, a friend of mine was forced to take leave from leading his corporation due to a nervous breakdown he suffered after the financial collapse of his organization. His problems were the result of poor management. He knew he could never recover on his own, so he searched for someone to help him find his way through the ruins of what remained. He was grateful to find a trusted leader who embraced him in his brokenness and a therapist who walked him through the emotional and spiritual maze back to wholeness. He finished his career with honorable success and dignity.

In spite of the church's efforts to confront broken lifestyles, we still take exit ramps that lead to a dead end. The embarrassment we have suffered before the world has done little to discourage our choices. While the media especially enjoys exposing skeletons in the closets of high-profile people, the humiliation has not provoked us to flee snares that lead us astray. Books, seminars and ministries have emerged to help heal family breakdowns, curtail divorce rates and encourage morals. Somehow we think we will be the exception. We discover, however, we are no different from anyone else. In spite of our attempts to rein ourselves in, failures still happen at an alarming rate. Failure is not, however, the end of the story. It does not have to be the end of your story.

THE FAILURE AND THE FALLEN

I've often thought how the church appears so embarrassed over the appalling failures among our own that we forget the fallen ones themselves. Somehow God had a perfect balance — He always does. God is more concerned about the bruised and beaten person who fell and those wounded from his fall than the incident that took place.

Religion typically reacts with disgust when people break God's laws. God, however, sees broken people, *rather than* the broken rule. He does not turn away from our brokenness even when we are at fault. Scripture says, *"The Word became flesh and blood, and moved into the neighborhood"* (John 1:14, Message). Consider that He knew all along the neighborhood He was moving into wasn't that great. Compared to where He came from, He moved into the "hood" — next door to all of us, dysfunctional, messed-up people.

After Adam and Eve disobeyed God and ate the fruit of the forbidden tree, Scripture records that God came asking, *"Where are you?"*

(Genesis 3:9). His first concern was not the broken command, but His broken people. After He helped them locate themselves, He then confronts their problem. *"What is this you have done?"* (Genesis 3:13).

The tender heart of God looked for His wounded loved ones *before* bringing up the issue that caused their fall in the first place. In spite of blatantly yielding to the word of the serpent over His word, the Father's primary concern was for Adam and Eve. He first reaches for us who become crippled by our own defiant choices then deals with the repercussions of our waywardness. Love does this, and since *God is love* (1 John 4:8, 16), this is what He does because this is who He is.

After confronting Adam and Eve with the consequences of their sin, God lovingly *"made tunics of skin, and clothed them"* (Genesis 3:21). God is a Restorer who would not leave them uncovered to expose their shame. He protects them with a sacrifice, covering Adam and Eve with the skin of an animal still dripping with blood. This act was a prophetic shadow of the sacrifice of our Lord Jesus Christ who would later be the ultimate sacrifice by shedding His blood on the cross.

It's not wise to compromise Scripture's instruction to live a holy life, nor should we neglect to hold one another to biblical standards of character. On the other hand, we dare not push those who have fallen to the side without hope of coming back into relationship with God and the assignment He has for their lives. God is a God of the rebound. In His kingdom, failure, no matter how gruesome, is never the end of the game. Failure never has the last word.

When God's people, Israel, fell into idolatry He never gave up on them. Even before they acknowledged their blatant rebellion, the Lord prepared for their return. When neighboring nations saw Israel as weak and hopeless, God revealed they would rebound to their place of influence among the nations of the world. We have a superior covenant to that of the Old Testament and possess greater hope to return to our place before we erred from our purpose. We have been given hope for a full recovery from our failures, to rebound into the God-called mission for our lives.

It's heartbreaking to see some of our most significant warriors collapse. They often live with a limited expectation of fulfilling God's original plan for their lives. Many of them are hopeless because we have not been sure we could or should offer them the prospect of a full recovery. The fallen are often shuffled off to a counselor's office with hopes that they will pick up the pieces of what's left of their lives and move on. If their failure publicly embarrassed us, it's often hoped that time will erase the humiliation they caused. This scenario should not be, and it does not have to be, the outcome.

God Himself once looked upon His failure-ridden people and lamented, *"No one says, 'Restore'!"* (Isaiah 42:22). Can you sense the disappointment in the tone of that statement? He is grieved that no one would lift a voice and sound a prophetic decree, *"Restore!"* over His fallen people.

Rebounding from failure involves three actions. First, those who fell need to acknowledge responsibility for their part in the failure, if indeed there is any. Second, someone prophetically declares, *"Restore,"* the game is not over, and a rebound is possible. Third, and most important, action must be taken. Faith to walk it out is necessary. Though it's not laid out in this order, this book will lead you through this process.

God instated the rebound into the game of life. This rebound is nothing less than restoration from failure to the purpose and destiny He planned from the beginning.

A FAILED SHOT AND A FAMOUS REBOUND

I've often wondered what the game of basketball would be like without the rebound. With the action taken out of the game, players would only take turns shooting the ball at the goal and settle for a boring game of HORSE. The rebound keeps the game alive after someone has missed the target.

Perhaps one of the most renowned rebounds of all time took place in 1983 at the NCAA championship game. It was no surprise the University of Houston led by Akeem Olajuwon and Clyde Drexler finished the tournament as one of the final two teams. But the basketball world was dazed when a Cinderella squad from North Carolina State University, with barely more regular season wins than losses, faced the Houston powerhouse for the national title. Even more stunning, NC State won the championship after someone on the team missed a shot.

With the score tied and five seconds left in the game, NC State's guard Derek Whittenburg hurled the ball toward the basket from thirty-five feet away. It fell short, but NC State center Lorenzo Charles rebounded the airball and dunked it into the goal for a dazzling two-point championship win. The unforgettable image of the rebound and dunk, with State's coach Jimmy Valvano running in circles looking for someone to hug, would be aired on television for decades as one of college basketball's greatest moments.

Because of the rebound, the failed shot was not the end of the game, but the beginning of a victory. In fact, the failed shot followed by the rebound made North Carolina State's win that much sweeter.

Your failure was not the end of your game either. It's my aim to help you understand that when you missed the target God grabbed the rebound that keeps you in the game. If you'll allow me to, I'll walk with you until you get another shot at fulfilling your purpose and destiny. The final buzzer has not sounded. You're still in the game.

SUPERNATURAL ENCOUNTERS FOR THE JOURNEY

I was raw and bloody from moral collapse and unsure of whether someone like me could return. Through a supernatural encounter God encouraged me in my journey. It happened when my wife and I were at a shopping center walking into a grocery store. On a late Saturday afternoon in June, the parking lot was full of cars with most people attending the movie theater next door.

As I got out of our car, I caught a glimpse of a beautiful, fully restored 1956 Chevy. Its bright red paint job, custom reupholstered interior, shiny chrome rims and supercharged engine towering out of the hood made it hard to miss. It was an impressive machine.

To appreciate this story you need to know I grew up around these muscle cars. As a boy coming up in the late sixties and seventies, my dad was the neighborhood mechanic who specialized in '55, '56 and '57 Chevys. Dad was a "Chevrolet guy," as opposed to a "Ford guy" (apologies to the Ford guys). I think I saw the guts of every 283, 327, 396, 409 and 427 engine Chevrolet ever manufactured in those days. Spotting the bright red gas-guzzler scratched a nostalgic itch.

As we walked into the grocery store the words "That's a great looking car, isn't it?" flew through my mind.

At first, I treated the thought as only a "thought" until I heard, "You should have seen what it looked like before I restored it."

I stopped dead in my tracks right in the middle of the produce section beside the apples and bananas. I knew this to be the Lord's voice.

I hardly noticed my wife filling the shopping cart because all I could think about was, "You should have seen what it looked like *before I restored it.*" The words replayed in my mind. Over and over I heard *"before I restored it—before I restored it—before I restored it."* I knew it was God speaking because it was too creative to be me.

How did it look before? I wondered. Did the restorer pull it out of someone's backyard? Was it beat up and rusty? The more I considered it, the more encouraged I became. I wasn't aware of it yet, but God was proclaiming, *"Restore!"* over my life.

As we exited the store, there she sat, still turning heads of those who passed by.

When I looked at it, the Lord spoke again. "Bill, I want you to know this '56 Chevy has a better paint job, better tires and wheels, the interior is more elaborate, and it has a more powerful engine than it did when the original owner drove it home."

I could hardly contain myself, but there was more.

"Out of all the hundreds of shiny new cars in this parking lot that have never had a ding or dent, everyone's eyes remain riveted to the restored car."

"Bill," He said, "This car is worth more today than it was the day it rolled off the showroom floor."

On the surface, I appeared to be a typical unenthusiastic husband pushing a shopping cart, but inside I was doing cartwheels.

"I get it, Lord!" I shouted under my breath.

The restored '56 Chevy brings several lessons with it.

First, when someone restores a car in this way, it's considered to be "modified." Restored people are, indeed, modified and custom made for the future that lies ahead for them. We will be who we were, and yet different. But, rest assured, the difference will be appealing because restored people display the beauty of God's redemption.

Second, restored people turn heads and seize people's attention, especially from those who know what we have come through. Our rebound astounds everyone who sees in us a gleaming example of God's grace.

Finally, people restored from failure beautifully portray God's redeeming character. His redemption, mercy and grace make us more valuable in our restored state than we were before we wrecked our lives.

You should know one important fact about my encounter with the '56 Chevy. Like the Chevy, I was born in 1956. While God never shortened my journey, He gave me small, supernatural encounters that kept me encouraged when I felt like giving up. While you may not have the same types of experiences, the Holy Spirit will be just as personal with you as you rebound to your purpose and destiny in God.

Jeremiah's often quoted promise to wayward Israel was, *"For I know the plans I have for you, declares the Lord, plans for welfare and not for evil, to give you a future and a hope"* (Jeremiah 29:11). Your heavenly Father has not abandoned you or His plans for you. He will give windows of hope along the way. You may not immediately see the whole pathway, but God will provide enough light for you to take the next step. When you take action the road will unfold as you move along by faith.

This Is Not Cheap Grace

I'm not promoting cheap grace. Rebounding and being restored demand the development of Christ-like character. At times the way may appear to be narrow, but it's the best way and, most definitely, God's way.

A new breed of people is coming forth who will boldly declare, *"Restore!"* over those that others have counted out. They know it's possible for the most significant failures in the eyes of men to come back to an intimate relationship with God and rebound as champions to fulfill their dreams, destiny and purpose. What God planned for you before your fall awaits your return.

In my first book *He Restores* I targeted fallen leaders who are no longer fulfilling God's call upon their lives. Over time, however, I met ordinary people, who, for various reasons, lost their way because of failure. They were eager to get back into the game of life, but after repeated disappointments they just weren't sure if it was possible.

I found homemakers, mechanics, teachers, wealthy and the not-so-wealthy sitting on the sidelines because they failed at some place in their journey. What they all had in common was the memory of a faith that used to be alive and a purpose that gave them a reason to get up in the morning. They questioned if life could be the same after a collapse such as theirs.

The principles outlined in these chapters are spiritual arsenals drawn from Scripture and personal experience. They are as relevant to heads-of-state as they are to the heads-of-a-household. These lessons were pounded out in real life, and by God's grace I am one who has lived to talk about it. For, you see, I too am a restored version of my original self.

I know what it's like to be the beloved star player. And I know how it feels to miss the mark and have the crowds jeer in disappointment. I also know, after sitting on the bench, the joy of getting back in the game and putting up a score.

I wish I could say I lived these principles out by hearing, submitting and obeying, but I cannot. I came to these conclusions the hard way, by trying to devise a comeback on my terms. In His mercy, God pressed me to abandon my plan and embrace His. God loved me enough to allow the consequences of my choices to break me until I surrendered to His will. And in case you're wondering, He loves you enough to do the same thing with you.

God has not abandoned you or His plans for you. He has made provision for everyone who sits in the shadows questioning if they've let their best days slip away. The God who created you has not given up on you, and if He hasn't who are you to give up on yourself?

You hold in your hands a prophetic decree to encourage and direct you. Consider this a statement to the church, society as a whole, but especially to everyone who sits idly by because of one or more repeated failures. As you begin the process of rebounding to the purpose and destiny for your life, I declare the Father's heart over you.

"Restore!"

Chapter Two

Can I Live Again?

I don't want to stand before God and have Him ask me why I chose to die before I stopped breathing.

The most vulnerable people on earth are those who live with an unbridled passion for excelling in their life's purpose. That statement may puzzle you because passionate people more often appear invincible, rather than vulnerable. Some of these influencers have immense followings leading large organizations, corporations or churches. And yet some among this unique breed bear neither a heady title nor position. Their lives merely spill over to inspire people around them to embrace God's best to be all they were created to be.

Unlike the individual who lives day-to-day with no thought of impacting their world, these people know our lives matter. Their tenacity possibly explains why they become targets for spiritual assaults. Satan knows if he can remove one of these gallant warriors he will dissuade many from pursuing their own purpose in God.

Far too many of this noble class have been paralyzed and set aside because they fell in battle. Families, businesses, churches, even nations suffer from their absence. They often live the balance of their lives on the fringes, never returning to fulfill their purpose and do what they're gifted to do. Losing them could mean losing the inspiration for the likes of a prophet Samuel, a General Patton, Winston Churchill or another Billy Graham.

INVISIBLE FOE AND TANGIBLE LOSSES

The Bible holds one of the oldest pieces of literature, sand-wiched between the story of Queen Esther and the psalms of King David. It's the dramatic tale of a good man's influence, his losses and, at last, his return. The book bears the title of the story's leading character known as Job.

It opens by telling us God highly esteemed Job, more so than any other person on the earth. There was, however, a downside to this honor. Satan took notice of Job too. He pointed out Job's immense wealth, but it wasn't that alone that caught Satan's eye. Job lived with the favor of God on his life which was what Satan himself lusted for when he served as the high cherub, Lucifer, at the throne of God (see Isaiah 14:12-14).

> *"Then the Lord said to Satan, 'Have you considered my servant Job, that there is none like him on the earth, a blameless and upright man, one who fears God and shuns evil'"* (Job 1:8).

This favor stirred the wrath of Satan against Job. *"Does Job fear God for nothing?"* (Job 1:9). Such jealousy is the devil's response to everyone who bears the favored seal of the Holy Spirit. He accuses us of loving God for the benefits alone.

> *"But now, stretch out **Your** hand and touch all that he has, and he will surely curse You to Your face!"* (Job 1:11, bold added).

By challenging God, Satan reveals his deception. *"Stretch out **Your** hand."* He knew God's character, that He would not stretch out His hand against His loved one. In His great wisdom God permits Satan, albeit with limits, to stretch out his own hand against Job.

> *"And the Lord said to Satan, 'Behold, all that he has is in your power; only do not lay a hand on his person'"* (Job 1:12).

We still confuse the hand of Satan with the hand of God. We often mistake our battles in life as a sign of God's displeasure when they are just the opposite. God knew Job loved Him more than the possessions He had given him, even more than his own family. An unseen conflict was in the making, and Job was the prized trophy. Indeed, the season ahead would be painful for Job, but God had a plan for the other side of Job's pain. What would appear to be a massive defeat would become one of the supreme victories recorded in eternities past.

Satan attacked Job by hiding in the daily battles of life. Concealed guerilla warfare is one of the devil's greatest schemes. Chapter 1 of Job tells how raiders from neighboring nations suddenly appear and kill his servants and livestock. Then two natural disasters destroy the remaining sheep, servants, his children and houses. Job's response? *"He fell to the ground and worshiped"* (Job 1:20). To rub salt in the devil's wound, it says, *"In all this Job did not sin nor charge God with wrong"* (Job 1:22).

Never forget these things happened *because* of God's favor. Many of the conflicts we face are due to God's favor upon us, not His disapproval of us. Even so, if we fail in the fight, and many of us do, a right response can turn defeats into victories. Job lost everything, and it looked as if he either failed God or God abandoned him. Smoke swirled above the ashes of their smoldering homes, and stalls once populated with livestock now stood empty. Job's response, however, was the winning blow. He humbled himself and *"fell to the ground and worshiped."* Scene 1 of this ageless encounter closes when Job lands a surprising punch called "humility." Round 1 ends with the score, Job–1, Satan–0.

God doesn't keep score as we do. Humility positions failures on earth to stand as champions before God. The winning punch is the attitude they choose. In all their shortcomings they have God, and so they worship Him in spite of their losses.

The battle was not over. In fact, it was only beginning. Because Job worshipped, Satan pushed back at him harder still. Satan challenged God: *"Stretch out **Your hand** now, and touch his bone and his flesh, and he will surely curse You to Your face!"* (Job 2:5, bold added). God accepts the challenge with one exception; He would still not use His hand to harm His loved one. He tells Satan, *"Behold, he is in your hand, but spare his life"* (Job 2:6). As before, Satan hid in the natural and brought sickening boils upon Job's body from head to toe.

Looking back on his prosperous days intensified Job's fight. He reminisced,

> *"When I went to the city and took my seat in the public square, the young men saw me and stepped aside, and the old men rose to their feet. . . . I chose the way for them and sat as their chief; I dwelt as a king among his troops"* (Job 29:7-8, 25, NIV).

Such are the regrets of one who has lost his standing among those who were once inspired by his life. Interestingly, Job never openly mourns the loss of his children and personal possessions. Could it be he mourned the loss of his purpose in life more than the loss of children and property? I suppose it's something we'll never know. We do know, however, Job's standing with God and influence with men made him a trophy the devil wanted to add to his collection. The direct hit of one tragedy after another so affected Job's confidence that even his wife and a few remaining friends questioned his character. The enemy intended to make him a byword of shame to those who once revered him. Satan was allowed to strip him of his children, possessions and health. Satan's ultimate goal? He wanted Job to curse God and die.

Job's losses mounted. Possessions, children, reputation, his position at the city gate and now his health—gone. He appeared and felt nothing like the champion he was destined to become. Job bowed lower still. Humility, once again, was the weapon Job raised against his adversary. He humbled himself and declared, *"Shall we indeed accept good from God, and shall we not accept adversity?"* (Job 2:10).

Heaven smiles, as I imagine glorious angels swooping down in the Olympian fashion, raising banners to declare the actual status of the contest. Round 2 comes to an end, and it's Job–2, Satan–0.

14

People who are a threat to demonic strongholds are targets for sin that can prevent them from fulfilling their purpose. The authority they once employed in families, churches, corporations and governments suffer when these men and women fall and remain on the sidelines of failure.

We are entering an era when helping fallen soldiers to rebound is taken more seriously. In past decades, we staggered at the numbers of people in corporate, political and church circles who disqualified themselves from service by their failures. In the coming years, however, we will be equally astounded by the restoration of those who, in humility, return to fulfill their purpose and destiny. Men and women in various circles will rebound, fully restored to achieve their purpose in the earth.

Is There Life after Failure?

At his lowest point, Job asks the question we all ask: *"If a man dies, shall he live again?"* (Job 14:14). Job wanted to know, "Is there hope for me to be productive again? Is it possible to come back from such personal devastation?"

Not only did Job lose his children, wealth and health, but his lowly state of life caused him to lose his influence as well. The people closest to him assumed the worst and prophesied his doom. Everyone considered him beyond the point of return.

I understand this question all too well. To lose your purpose and be denied your destiny feels like death. Once you have given yourself to pursue your life's purpose, you will never be satisfied with merely making a living and paying the bills. You want to live again, and that means fulfilling your mission to impact and inspire others for good. It feels as if a death sentence is issued against you when the right to fulfill your purpose slips away.

By Now We Stink

Consider Lazarus, one of Jesus' closest friends. He had lain in a grave four days before the Master came to his aid. Lazarus's sister Mary complained that if Jesus had arrived sooner He could have healed her brother as He did so many others. In Mary's thinking, now that Lazarus had died, all hope of his ever living a full life had vanished. Lazarus lay buried in a sealed tomb, complete with mourners and a funeral procession in place. No one imagined seeing him alive again.

Looking into the tomb and lifting his voice to command the dead man, Jesus ordered Lazarus to come out. His body had begun to deteriorate and stink, but that didn't matter to Jesus. A walking dead man would be a good advertisement for the living God.

In the same way, the circumstances surrounding those of us who have miserable failures to our account are usually just as messy and smelly as a four-day-old dead man. By the time we realize our real condition, like Lazarus, we stink. Herein lies the inevitable question. Is it possible for those who have fallen so low, after "stinking up" their lives, to be restored to their former purpose and destiny? Can a person rebound and have a second chance, a do-over, in life?

I want to remind you how Jesus used resurrections to draw attention to an excellent Father who takes great pleasure in raising the dead. Just as He used Lazarus's resurrection to bring people to God, He plans to do the same with you. God unashamedly calls the names of those buried in tombs of failure because some of His most fruitful followers arise from the graveyards of life.

When Purpose Is Lost

I have been at the forefront of a group of people, large and small, in some capacity since I was fifteen years old. It started in high school on athletic teams and continued throughout my high school years. My classmates chose me to be president of my classes, including the student body president my senior year. After graduation, I gave my life to Christ, surrendered to a call to ministry and at twenty-one began leading a church. I have been an influencer at the helm of a group of people most of my life.

At a pinnacle of successful leadership, I fell, and it was ugly. Sin always makes us look ugly as if God has rejected us. On the contrary, our frailty is what endears us to Him more than we realize.

Losing my influence and livelihood, I planned my comeback. Like so many do, I made the mistake of thinking I would confess my mistakes—well, some of them anyway—and pick up right where I left off. I was wrong. Like Israel in Jeremiah's day, it took time for me to discover the disaster I created. The wound was more profound than I imagined, and I was more deceived than I realized. People expressed little hope for me to have a future that even remotely mirrored my past.

I would read books by authors who boldly stated no failure was final. And yet hope evaporated each time I replayed in my mind what I had done. Like the lost son Jesus talked about in Luke 15, I was slowly coming to grips with the seriousness of my failure and wondered if I would return from my far country.

"But they don't know how sinful and deceiving I've been," I confessed to myself. "If the writer (referring to the author of the book I was reading at the time) knew my situation, they would agree my case is different." Doubt confined me to a grave of failure, and I saw no way out.

Though it's not always the case, much of the time sin is involved in a failure. At the least, some deception is the cause of our mistakes and misjudgments. In Christian circles we refer to this as a "fall." Furthermore, Scripture states that sin *"brings forth death"* (James 1:15). It's not uncommon to witness the death of reputation, family, marriage, business, ministries, relationships, and the list is endless. On a personal level, there's the death of dreams and purpose, not to mention self-esteem and confidence.

HELPING PEOPLE REBOUND IS THE TASK OF THE CHURCH

Our approach in assisting people to rebound and be restored should be the same as our approach to any other ministry. Just as we intentionally reach out to people with any need, we are to restore those who have lost their way—and even those who have repeatedly lost their way and have come back to try again.

Galatians 6:1 states, *"Brethren, if a man is overtaken in any trespass, you who are spiritual restore such a one in a spirit of gentleness, considering yourself lest you also be tempted."* This passage lays out a process for us to follow.

- *"If a man is overtaken."* The ESV reads, *"If anyone is caught."* We restore, not only those who confess but also the ones found in the act of their chaos that's causing the problem.
- *"Any trespass."* No sin is too great for the restoring power of God's mercy.
- *"You who are spiritual."* Those who have this revelation to restore and rebound a fallen friend will be the ones to lead the way. Some even possess a gift for such a ministry.
- *"Restore."* The word means "to return to the place they were before they failed." Or to say it another way, "rebound."
- *"You. . .restore such a one."* The implication is that the church, God's people of faith, is expected to restore the fallen.
- *"Spirit of gentleness."* Compassion is the posture from which we restore those who are wounded by their own actions or the acts of others against them.
- *"Lest you too be tempted."* The apostle Paul reminds us no one is beyond some level of failure. With this in mind, humility should accompany the ministry of restoration. Humility, as I have said, is always the winning blow against our enemy.

Again, consider Lazarus. The people standing near his grave wanted no part of Jesus' compassion for His dead friend. They were apprehensive about his stench. When Jesus told them to remove the stone, they reacted harshly and responded, *"By this time there is a stench"* (John 11:39).

Jesus called Lazarus out of his tomb, and he was very much alive but still *"bound hand and foot with grave clothes, and his face wrapped in a cloth"* (John 11:44a). It's a fact that after four days dead people have an odor. And I'm sure the graveclothes of Lazarus who had been dead and buried four days were pungent. So what does Jesus do? He elicits the help of those standing around and makes Lazarus's rebound a community project.

Lazarus was entirely alive and yet still limited because of his time in the grave. So Jesus does something brilliant as the onlookers watch this mummified man attempt to walk out. He instructs the very people who feared his stench to *"loose him, and let him go"* (John 11:44). The people Jesus picked to restore Lazarus to full functionality were those who were opposed to opening his grave because they detested his smell.

I often wonder how many resurrected failures are still not walking out their God-given purpose because no one has loosed them from their past. Religion has taught us to steer clear from associating with those who reek from failure lest we appear to condone their past behavior. Sadly, some within the community of faith abhor the lingering smell of the grave. Others stand at a distance for fear the stench will get on them by association. Isn't it strange that Jesus faced the same problem and baffled the religious community when He ate with sinners and tax collectors? Those with a questionable stench loved being with Jesus because He did not treat them like second-class grave dwellers. Even after all they had done, Jesus gave them hope of living the life God intended for them all along.

THE ROAD BACK BEGINS WITH HUMILITY

Desiring a retreat for prayer, I remembered the local Episcopal church always left the doors of their chapel unlocked for people looking for a sacred and warm refuge. In despair late one night, I walked into the tiny chapel and collapsed at the altar. Confessing out loud—*very loud*, in fact—I called out to God everything I could think of that contributed to my failure. Before that night I had superficially acknowledged my wrong actions and behavior. But I had only gone through the motions, saying what I thought people expected me to say. Looking back, I was more concerned with pacifying people than allowing God to change my heart.

19

This particular night, however, my confession came up out of a deep well in my soul. I was surprised to hear myself asking God to reveal everything to me I had kept hidden. I lay face down on the burgundy carpet in front of the shiny brass cross at the altar. While lying prostrate, God's voice broke through my tears and sobs. It wasn't audible, and yet it was crystal clear.

"The last chapter of your life has not been written."

I don't recall ever having heard this phrase before God spoke to me that night. And just as He said, the last chapter had not been written. In fact, one reason my story continues is to assure you that neither have you reached the final episode of your life.

He Restores

Weeks later, with my Bible in my lap, I sat at my bedroom window occasionally glancing down at Psalm 23. My eyes became riveted to verse 3: *"He restores my soul."* While reading, I had a strange vision. What appeared to be a round magnifying glass appeared over this verse. As you know, if you magnify something it is enlarged, and you lose part of it as the size increases. It was as if the magnifying glass positioned itself over the verse so the only words left visible were *"He restores."*

Once again, God had spoken. He wanted to settle the issue and assure me of His willingness to restore people like me. God will restore anyone once we've submitted ourselves to Him, and this includes *you*.

If a Man Dies, Shall He Live Again?

"If a man dies, shall he live again?" Job's question demands an answer. I've discovered the answer is conditional. It depends on whether you're honest about what took place in your life and how willing you are to make proper steps in moving forward. I'm a testimony of a Job who lost everything and a resurrected Lazarus that reeked of death. After all these years, God's mercy continues to wipe away the stench of the graveclothes I wore for too long.

Can you live again? Absolutely. And, indeed, you must. In fact, it's imperative for others that you rebound to life and remain in the game. Consider this a roadmap with landmarks showing you the way forward. But before you move on I want you to settle the issue that God is a good Father who restores. Rebounds are part of His game plan. You will discover in the next chapter that restoring us from failure is one of the primary concerns on His heart.

Chapter Three

The God Who Pursues

It has been said we have a God-shaped vacuum in our hearts only God can fill. I believe this to be true. There is, however, a truth more mysteriously grand than this. There's a human-shaped vacuum in God's heart only we can fill. He never relents in His quest to capture us with His love and fill the place that's made just for us.

In an ideal environment and perfect world, Adam and Eve fell. Immediately God resolved to restore them and everything affected by their failure. Their failure came because they believed the lie of God's archenemy, that serpent we know as Satan. The story of man's great failure became known as "the fall of man."

Before Adam could hardly get the forbidden fruit swallowed, God declared Satan's doom. But what's more astounding, He promised to restore everything Adam lost from his failure, including the fallen ones themselves. Even more surprising, God declared He would use the first one to disobey His command, the woman, to bring about Satan's final defeat.

After their fall, God pursues His beloved man and woman. Fearing a dreaded confrontation, Adam and Eve go into hiding from their Divine Lover. What would God now do after entrusting His entire creation into their care? How would He react to such a devastating failure that would eventually affect not only their immediate family but the whole human race?

First, God asks Adam, *"Have you eaten from the tree of which I commanded you that you should not eat?"* (Genesis 3:11). Adam admits, *"I ate"* (Genesis 3:12). Then to Eve, He asks, *"What is this you have done?"* (Genesis 3:13a). Eve also confesses, *"I ate"* (Genesis 3:13b). What follows is God's stunning reaction to their confession of failing and falling.

Turning to the ultimate culprit, the devilish serpent, God declares, *"Because you have done this, **you are cursed**"* (Genesis 3:14, bold added). Standing between the devil and the woman, God Himself prophesies, *"I will put enmity between you* [Satan] *and the woman, and between your seed and her seed; He shall bruise your head, and you shall bruise His heel"* (Genesis 3:15). Immediately following Eve's confession of failure, God declared "Restore" (see Isaiah 42:22) over their lives. In spite of Eve's disobedience, God did not wash His hands from using the woman again. In fact, the ones whose failure had a domino effect on every person to be born after them, God rebounded. He would use the seed and offspring of woman to deliver all humanity from the fallout of their sin. Jesus Christ did not merely appear from heaven. *"God sent forth His Son, **born of a woman**"* (Galatians 4:4, bold added).

God's heart is to restore us from our dreaded ruins and return us to fulfill our ultimate purpose and destiny. He did not do this only for Adam and Eve but for us, too. From the beginning of time God is a God of the rebound.

What would our Bible look like if Scripture only contained Genesis 1 and 2 and our first parents' immense failure in Genesis 3 had never occurred? Essentially, humanity's history of sin and strife recorded throughout the pages of the Bible would not exist. Following Genesis 1 and 2, our story would conclude with the book of the Revelation, chapters 21 and 22, with every nation, tongue and tribe worshipping God in the heavenly Jerusalem. Therefore, everything from Genesis 3 to Revelation 20 is an account of God pursuing His people to restore us to our original purpose before Adam and Eve's great failure. The first two chapters of Genesis and the last two chapters of Revelation are our story without the failure in the garden known as the "the fall of man."

Out of all His creation Adam and Eve were the only objects of God's love from which He desired their love in return. In the middle of the garden God placed a tree called *"the tree of the knowledge of good and evil"* (Genesis 2:9, 17) and forbade them to eat from it. Obeying would reflect their love of God. After all, love must have a choice not to love, in order to be true love. The Lord commanded Adam, *"But of the tree of the knowledge of good and evil you shall not eat, for in the day that you eat of it you shall surely die"* (Genesis 2:17).

The conclusion of Genesis 2 is like a surreal prose, what some might call a fairy tale. *"And they were both naked, the man and his wife, and were not ashamed"* (Genesis 2:25). I imagine this to be a time when Adam had his most intimate conversations with God. He had nothing to hide. Adam's relationships were unhindered as he enjoyed perfect communion with God, his wife and all of creation.

Restored from the Fall

Had Adam not failed, we would have a perfect story. But he did, and the account in Genesis 3 stands opposed to creation's ideal design. To this day, Adam and Eve's failure not only affected them but all of God's creation. Consequently, Scripture tells us that creation groans with anticipation of the full redemption of the sons of God (see Romans 8:19-22).

In different degrees, we all have a *before* (Genesis 1 and 2) and *after* (Genesis 3) story. Adam's fall (Genesis 3) is a reflection of all of us. It's this seed of failure lurking within our hearts that entices us to eat from forbidden trees. Our forbidden tree, whatever it may be for us, is the seedbed of our personal Genesis 3 experience.

Like Adam, while we can't undo the events of our past, God pursues us to reverse the effects. I desire that you know the heart of a Father who does not stand aloof, shaking His head as if you had your chance but blew it. Instead, He pursues you to restore everything you lost from your failures. Our God has set His heart on pursuing you with His love and will not give up until He restores you to your original beauty and purpose.

ON THE REBOUND

The words *rebound* and *restore* have similar meanings. Both refer to recovering, returning and repairing what was lost, missed or misplaced. Both words convey hope to remain on the courts of life and finish with a victory. When life has unraveled, it's right and honorable for us to desire to rebound and complete our race.

For this writing, "rebounding" (being restored) means *to be healed in spirit, soul and body from our brokenness, no matter how we became broken. We are loosed from our past, free in our present and liberated to fulfill our assigned purpose for our future.*

The Bible reveals God as a loving Father patiently helping us through our blunders and brokenness. We will encounter twists and turns and many sub-points along the journey to the desired destination. Someone has said that life is not a straight horizontal timeline from beginning to end. Instead, it's filled with detours along the way. If we graphed our lifelines, we would find them zigging and zagging, going here and there, back and forth, rather than a perfect line from beginning to end. Though our purpose may at times become blurry to us, God never loses sight of it for it originated with Him when He created us. He knows where we should end up, and He's committed to helping us arrive there.

After Adam's failure I'm glad God didn't say, "Okay, buddy, you've blown it! You had your chance. From here on, you're on your own." Instead of washing His hands of Adam and Eve, God declared His intention to use them to fulfill His purpose on the earth. The first one deceived, the woman would give birth to One who would restore everything they lost. After Adam fell, God didn't abandon him but pursued him with the intention to use his failure to demonstrate the depth of His love for His people. God seeks you just because He loves you. Period.

THE END WILL BE GREATER

Throughout the Old Testament, Israel turned away from following God more times than you can count. Because of their rebellion, they lost their esteem among the nations that once revered and feared them. The Lord, however, never lost sight of His plan to restore them to their respected place. Even when He sent judgment upon them, He did it with a plan to bring them back. Jeremiah 33:7-9 records,

> *"And I will cause the captives of Judah and the captives of Israel to return, and will rebuild those places as at the first.*
>
> *"I will cleanse them from all their iniquity by which they have sinned against Me, and I will pardon all their iniquities by which they have sinned and by which they have transgressed against Me.*
>
> *"Then it shall be to Me a name of joy, a praise, and an honor before all nations of the earth, who shall hear all the good that I do to them; they shall fear and tremble for all the goodness and all the prosperity that I provide for it."*

It's as if God declares that His people will be better after He restores them from their disgrace than they were before they failed Him. It doesn't mean He makes light of our sin and failure. It does say, however, that our faults never provoke God to trash His original purpose and plan for our lives. In spite of our shortcomings, He's committed to revealing His goodness and glory through us.

The prophets announced God's promise to restore Israel. Haggai 2:9 declares, *"The glory of this latter temple shall be greater than the former."* His people had neglected their spiritual welfare, but God still declared, *"The latter. . .shall be greater."* If this was true for Israel who lived under Old Testament law, it must be true for us who receive Jesus Christ as our Lord of grace.

THE FALL AND REBOUND OF THE ROCK

Does it get any worse than denying your friendship with the Lord? Jesus had extraordinary plans for Simon Bar-Jonah. Simon's destiny was so great that He changed his name to "Peter–*the Rock*" to signify the magnitude of his call. When pressed to live up to his name, Peter revealed he was anything but a rock.

Before the crucifixion of Jesus, as the Jewish council interrogated the Lord, Peter kept his distance warming by a fire. When a woman confronted him insisting he was a follower of the Nazarene, Peter answered her, *"I do not know Him"* (Luke 22:57). Not once, but three times, Peter flatly denied his intimate three-year friendship with Jesus. As Peter watched the Jewish leaders and the Roman soldiers flogging Jesus, he looks up to find his beaten friend gazing at him. Eye-to-eye with Jesus, Peter *"remembered the word of the Lord. . .and wept bitterly"* (Luke 22:61-62).

Remorse never looks worse than when we realize how we've chosen a path that has undermined our relationship with God and the people closest to us. The feeling of hopelessness is overwhelming. Can you imagine Peter's sickening emotion once he realizes he outright denied knowing Jesus? I can.

After the crucifixion Peter returns to fishing, the life he knew before he left to follow the Lord. Jesus, however, was not finished with Peter. While Peter was busy at work trying to catch fish, the resurrected Christ showed up waving to him from the shore. The scene took place after Christ had died on the cross and rose from the dead. Jesus had already grabbed the rebound from Peter's denial, and He had come to restore the fisherman to his divine purpose of fishing for men.

The scene of the resurrected Christ appearing to Peter after he returned to his old life feels eerily familiar. We who fall tend to believe our actions condemn us to the former life we once knew. God's love, however, is a pursuing love that hunts down those whom failure tries to doom.

"Simon. . .do you love Me?" (John 21:15). Three times, the same number he denied Him, Jesus asks Peter the question as He greets him on the shore. Jesus restored Peter with the invitation, *"Feed My*

sheep" (John 21:15-17). Peter is not only forgiven but also invited to return to the purpose of catching men for God's kingdom. Peter's life rebounds through the pursuing love of Jesus and the invitation to do what He called Peter to do from the beginning.

The Lord knows the exact words we need to hear to reignite faith and love. One word from God can do more to restore us than the many words of a counselor. Restoration is a process, but even so it begins with a simple invitation that awakens hope that God has not left us. He pursues us in spite of how badly we have failed Him.

Even Judas

Would it have been possible for the Lord to restore Judas Iscariot? Sounds unusual, I know. It's odd to envision Judas as a fully restored apostle. Before I offer an answer, let me pose another question. Have we not all, on some level, sold out for as little as thirty pieces of silver or less? To be honest, to save face from embarrassment, I've denied the Lord for the measly price of personal convenience. It's not uncommon for any of us to sell out to our fears. In the end, we look at the price we paid and realize, as Judas did, what a fool we have been.

Could Judas have come back? I believe he could have, but I'm not so sure Judas repented—even though before he hung himself, he regretted betraying innocent blood (see Matthew 27:3-4). After realizing the depth of his error, the devil convinced Judas his only option was suicide. It's not uncommon for believers, after repeated failures, to entertain suicidal thoughts. I've come to tell you God is pursuing you. The cross and resurrection of Jesus Christ rebounded your failure to restore you to the life He called you to all along. Judas never lived to see the resurrected Christ. You, however, have the record that bears witness that He came back from the grave to restore Peter and *you*.

REBOUNDING PRODIGALS

When a son or daughter falls, the Father grieves. God is a good Father who misses His children when they leave their place in the family. In Luke 15 Jesus relates the story of a younger son who left his father's household and fell into immoral living. Being the youngest son of an aristocratic family, the boy carried a certain degree of authority. Lured by an appetite for the other side of life, he rebels against his father and departs for a far country. You don't have to go that far to be far away. The far country speaks more about the distance of the heart than the location of a residence.

His older brother's attitude gives the impression he was not bothered about his younger brother's absence. The family business chugged right along with no one missing a beat. No one, that is, except the father. I see the dad sitting on the front porch of the home place looking for any sign of the boy's return. One day the old man thinks a distant speck on the horizon could be he. Indeed, it is his youngest son. Still a long way off, he can no longer stay put.

In his Gospel, Luke tells the story like this:

> *"And he arose and came to his father. But when he was still a great way off, his father saw him and had compassion, and ran and fell on his neck and kissed him.*
>
> *"And the son said to him, 'Father, I have sinned against heaven and in your sight, and am no longer worthy to be called your son.'*
>
> *"But the father said to his servants, 'Bring out the best robe and put it on him, and put a ring on his hand and sandals on his feet.*
>
> *"'And bring the fatted calf here and kill it, and let us eat and be merry; for this my son was dead and is alive again; he was lost and is found.' And they began to be merry"* (Luke 15:20-24).

It's one of the most vivid scenes in the Bible. Realizing what a fool he had been, the young boy heads for home, and yet he is still quite a distance away. Overwhelmed with joy that his son would chance a return, the father runs and greets him with hugs and kisses. Before the boy can demonstrate his sincerity or steps foot on the family estate, this loving dad restores his rebellious son threefold.

First, the best robe was brought to cover his appearance and disgusting odor. After losing a fortune on wild living, the only work he could find was on a pig farm, so he reeked of pigs. Under the Law of Moses, swine were unclean, and anyone who touched a pig became unclean. The boy had not only touched the pigs but lived with them for weeks. Even so, the father orders his servants to *"bring out the best robe."* The best robe, mind you, was the father's robe. With it, the dad would cover his young son's offensive smell and appearance. In spite of his disgusting behavior, this father was not about to make a spectacle of his son in front of the family and servants. The father's best robe covers the boy's broken condition. As he enters the house, he walks before family and friends arrayed in a garment of dignity and honor.

Second, the father placed the family signet ring on his finger and sandals on his feet. The ring was the symbol of restored authority and the shoes a sign of restored sonship. The family signet ring empowered the wearer to buy and sell in the family name. It was comparable to today's credit card. Imagine returning the family credit card to the one who wasted a fortune on wild living. Such is the heart of the God who rebounds and restores.

In ancient times slaves rarely wore shoes. Immediately they shod the boy with the sandals of sonship. No son of this father would walk around looking like a slave.

Finally, the father reasoned it was right to throw a party—a covenant meal to celebrate his son's return. Everyone joined in the celebration. Everyone, that is, but his older brother.

It's difficult for those who never leave the household to celebrate with the restored. Many who appear to be the faithful stumble over the extravagant love of their Father. It's hard for them to imagine their brothers and sisters having such favor after returning from lifestyles they lived in the far country.

THE WONDER OF THE CROSS

Bethlehem is the place where we first discover Immanuel, "God with us." As Phillips Brooks wrote in his beloved Christmas carol *O Little Town of Bethlehem*, this tiny town is where God fulfilled His promise to Eve, the first woman. In Bethlehem, *"The Word became flesh and dwelt among us"* (John 1:14). We celebrate Christmas as the occasion when God meets us on our level because we could never in a lifetime rise to meet His.

If the birth of Jesus is the celebration of God reaching down to us, the cross is where His persistent pursuit embraces us fully. Christ's death preceded His resurrection, and now the resurrected Christ sits beside the Father to intercede for us. He stands before God declaring, "That one, yes, the one who fell and failed miserably, she belongs to Me!" Love relentlessly pursues until it has apprehended its beloved. His love for you is why His pursuit is never-ending. In fact, I believe you are reading these words, not only because you seek Him, but because God is in pursuit of you.

The cross is a sign of God's forgiveness, but so much more. It displays His authority to bridge the gap that sin and failure create between God and us and, further, between us and His assigned purpose for our lives.

It's outrageous to think the sacrifice of Jesus Christ erases our rebellious deeds, past and present. Admittedly, this is not fair, but then grace never is. It's why Paul insisted, *"For the message of the cross is foolishness to those who are perishing, but to us who are being saved it is the power of God"* (1 Corinthians 1:18).

Don't skim over the words *"to us who are **being saved**."* These words mean we are always in process. As we live out this process called life, we will trip and fall along the way. Some failures will be worse than others. As I said, we will zig and zag our way along our journey. We can never complete the journey, however, without His grace. We were not only saved by grace (past), but grace is necessary for *"us who are **being saved**"* (present). God's grace in the cross of Christ is His eternal commitment empowering us to finish well. Grace is the difference maker!

When I Fall, I Will Arise

Fallen soldiers, especially those unaware of God's willingness to rebound our falls, are vulnerable to the taunts of the enemy. As he did Adam, the serpent lures us to defy the Lord's command then slithers off to leave us in our darkness. He wants us to feel that God has left us and that it's impossible for us to rise again. Behold the words of a minor prophet who carried a weighty word for fallen warriors:

> *"Do not rejoice over me, my enemy; **when I fall, I will arise**; when I sit in darkness, the Lord will be a light to me. I will bear the indignation of the Lord, because I have sinned against Him, until **He pleads my case** and executes justice for me. **He will bring me forth** to the light; I will see **His righteousness"*** (Micah 7:8-9, bold added).

The writer confesses his faults and does not sidestep his issues but willingly admits, *"I have sinned against Him."* And yet he knows the character of His God, and it's His character that empowers him to get up and try again.

Here is a beautiful decree of God's desire to pick up the fallen and rebound the failure. These declarations are to be made over your life as you open yourself to His grace. Grace enables you to respond rightly to God. *"When I fall, I will arise."* How do I dare to attempt to arise from my fall? Where do I get such authority to attempt a comeback? The prophet answers with, *"He pleads my case—**He** will bring me forth—I will see **His** righteousness."* I rebound because of God's grace, and His grace alone.

A Hostage of Hope

> *"As for you also, because of the blood of your covenant, I will set your prisoners free from the waterless pit. Return to the stronghold, you prisoners of hope.*

32

Even today I declare that I will restore double to you" (Zechariah 9:11-12).

We began our journey with God through the blood of Jesus Christ He shed on the cross. The book of the Revelation tells us our destination will come to an end at the throne of God and the Lamb (Revelation 22:3), the same Lamb that offered Himself on the cross. Our relationship to God, past, present and future, rests entirely upon the death and resurrection of Jesus Christ. I no longer put my hope in my performance, hoping, if given another chance, I will perform better. As I trusted Him to make me His son, I trust His grace to rebound my fall and help me finish well.

We're no longer prisoners of failure, but we have become a glorious hostage to hope. Imagine, if you can, being a *"prisoner of hope."* God's hope safely holds us until we are completely free from our emotional and spiritual baggage. It's *"because of the blood,"* which is His grace, that hope does its work until we celebrate our full freedom. While we wait we do so with expectation. "Expecting what?" you ask.

It's too good to imagine, but God promises to restore *double* to us all we lost from our foolishness. Whatever you suffered from failure, God will restore twice as much to those who devote themselves to Him. I say again, stop trying to figure out grace. It will never make sense to a mind that religion tries to justify through reason. Grace is not reasonable—it's wonderful.

The Bible is the story of a God who is a generous Father pursuing sons and daughters who have failed. This story, my friend, is *your story*. God has waited patiently for the chance to pursue you. And now, in His quest, He comes to apprehend you, not by condemnation, but by His love and kindness. At last, here you are, not ridiculed, but kissed, being fitted for a robe, a ring and shoes.

And why? Because *"this my son* [my daughter]. . .*is alive again."*

Chapter Four

Lord, Have Mercy

Mercy is the door of God's heart left open for a returning soul.

I t's possible to display a religious veneer, attend church, sing worship songs and still be far from God. Before we surrender to Him we have a natural bent toward sin that separates us from Him. Perhaps this is why, when we have fallen and failed so badly, we fear coming out in the open and baring ourselves to God. We are painfully aware of our nakedness. And this is why, if we have never encountered or understood God's mercy, we keep our distance because we fear rejection.

We are in quite a predicament because God is the only one who can deliver us from our plight. Our failures and often a continued struggle with the very thing that tripped us up to start with shame us into isolation. Any hopes of drawing nearer to God would be a sheer act of mercy. Fortunately, this is precisely where the gospel shines the brightest. God is always compassionate to the cry of His people for mercy.

As warmth is to a freezing man, God's mercy is to a fallen man. As a moth draws near to the light of a flame, we too are attracted to the One whose *"countenance is like the sun"* (Revelation 1:16). We discover, however, He also has *"eyes like a flame of fire"* (Revelation 1:14) that see the secrets of our hearts. Could it be that His eyes not only peer into the depths of our being to see the nakedness of our souls but to warm the souls as well? Mercy is God's heartwarming compassion laid upon the cold heart of failures like us.

When we are far from God and His purposes for our life, we rarely risk returning to Him until we know for sure He will receive us. Mercy is God's welcome mat that greets sons and daughters who have returned home from the far country.

MERCY'S DESCRIPTION

On this earth nothing compares with God's mercy. It is His compassion freely given to those who deserve the opposite. The Lord's mercy is an expression of His love, a love so extravagant we can offer nothing in return. Someone has said mercy is a greater One giving love and compassion to a lesser one. I suppose this is what makes it *mercy*.

Have you noticed we seek mercy when we are least deserving? We also hope God will withhold the consequences of our recklessness. Experience teaches us, however, that He does not withhold all the difficulties that come from the tares we have sown. Only time and eternity will reveal His wisdom and disclose just how much God withheld from the harvest of our craziness.

Scripture shows the universe is full of His limitless mercy, but it's also quite practical. We usually pray for mercy during hardship or crisis and rarely over trivial matters. Our need for compassion is life's emergency alarm, but we also need it as a daily necessity of life.

SEEKING GOD'S MERCY

The psalmists acknowledge our need for God's mercy in every possible place in life. They asked for mercy

- In times of weakness—Psalm 6:2
- When people cause trouble for us—Psalm 9:13
- Our sins—Psalm 25:7; 51:1
- In times of loneliness—Psalm 25:16

- In seasons of grief—Psalm 31:9
- When help was needed—Psalm 30:10
- When opposed by an enemy—Psalm 59:10
- In spiritual dryness and need for revival—Psalm 85:6-7
- When under the judgment of God—Psalm 85:4-7

The Lord's heart is tender toward the cry of His children asking for mercy. We often think of how undeserving we are, and after we have failed Him so badly, we ask, "Would God still be merciful to me?" Such a question is from a human perspective. The mystery of God's mercy can only be received, being far beyond human explanation. Remember: this is God's mercy, not ours. Our mercy has limits and conditions, but *"His mercy endures forever"* (Psalm 136).

While following Moses through the wilderness, the Israelites were prone to wander from God and worship idols. Even to those who willingly left Him, the heart of God could not resist their cry.

> *"Many times He delivered them; but they rebelled in their counsel, and were brought low for their iniquity.*
> *"Nevertheless He regarded their affliction, when He heard their cry;*
> *"And for their sake He remembered His covenant, and relented according to the multitude of His mercies"* (Psalm 106:43-45).

When God called Moses to lead Israel out of slavery, the Lord said, *"Behold, the cry of the children of Israel has come to Me"* (Exodus 3:9). More than a mere petition, they prayed in desperation. At some point, and only God knows where that is, the prayer became a *cry*. From their place of misery, God responded with mercy.

The New Testament contains the story of two blind men who were anxious to be healed when they heard Jesus was in their vicinity.

> *"When Jesus departed from there, two blind men followed Him, crying out and saying, 'Son of David, have mercy on us!' And when He had come into the house, the blind men came to Him. And Jesus said to*

*them, 'Do you believe that I am able to do this?' They
said to Him, 'Yes, Lord.' Then He touched their eyes,
saying, 'According to your faith let it be to you.' And
their eyes were opened"* (Matthew 9:27-30).

Once again, it was their cry for mercy that attracted Jesus' attention and ultimately gained their healing.

THE ABUNDANCE OF GOD'S MERCY

Believers become fugitives to their failures, unsure of God's mercy we once boldly believed. Before we risk being vulnerable before the Lord, we must have the assurance He will extend to us His boundless compassion. If that trust is not in our hearts, like Adam and Eve, we hide, fearful of exposing our nakedness.

Before his fall, Adam walked with God, but afterward the scene changes. God comes to Adam for His daily walk, and Adam is nowhere around. Instead of looking forward to His visit, Adam hides from perfect Love.

It would be wrong to assume God didn't know about Adam's failure. Obviously, He did. So we question, was he looking to punish them or to help them? Of course, it's the latter.

Often the church has taught that our fallenness so repulses God He would never draw near to us after we blatantly disobeyed Him. In Genesis 3, the garden scene reveals otherwise. Their fall would not keep God away from Adam and Eve. Instead, He drew near when they needed Him most.

It's no more possible for mercy to be absent from us than it is for heat to leave the sun. Mercy attaches itself to us in failure like steel to a magnet. Most times, however, we initially hide, not realizing our God is much better than we ever imagined Him to be. We "go underground," so to speak, because we're just not sure of His reaction to our choices that caused our fall.

It's true God detests sin. He is holy, and holiness abhors sin. When we choose sin, we erect a wall between God and us. *"Your iniquities have separated you from your God; and your sins have hidden His face from you, so that He will not hear"* (Isaiah 59:2). Religion often teaches that God raises a wall between us when He is displeased with our behavior. But God did not raise the wall. We did. The barrier sin erects, however, cannot stand when challenged by the gospel of Jesus Christ. Mercy is the good news of a God who positions Himself to pull down the wall and rebound us from failure.

In 1987 United States president Ronald Reagan stunned the world when he visited West Berlin, Germany. A physical wall known as "The Berlin Wall" had divided Western democracy from Eastern communism since 1961. Russia's Soviet Union controlled the barrier that kept millions of people from experiencing democracy's freedom. In a speech at the wall's famous Brandenburg Gate, President Reagan publicly challenged the Soviet Union's leader Mikhail Gorbachev. "Tear down this wall!" And so they did. For the first time in over a quarter of a century, millions of people in Eastern Europe would experience freedom.[1]

> *"But now in Christ Jesus you who once were far off have been brought near by the blood of Christ. For He Himself is our peace, who has made both one, and has broken down the middle wall of separation"* (Ephesians 2:13-14).

Sin is like a crimp in a water hose. Though connected to the source, it's possible to have something in between that stops the flow of life. Sin can be the crimp that puts a squeeze on the connection between the Divine Source and us. It's possible to be connected to our Source while an obstruction remains between Him and us. What's the answer?

The blood of Jesus Christ destroys walls, the "crimps," that allow God's life to flow to our need. At His death Jesus made a statement that had more significant implications than the one by President Reagan. *"It is finished"* (John 19:30). This statement proclaimed to the heavenly hosts, principalities and powers, humankind and all of the creation that Christ's death on the cross had once for all destroyed the wall that separated us from God. Through Christ's death and resurrection, mercy won the clash between our failures and God's holiness. *"We have been **made holy** through the sacrifice of the body of Jesus Christ once and for all"* (Hebrews 10:10, bold added).

THE PROTECTING POWER OF MERCY

Mercy is not merely an attitude, but a dominant force. As James 2:13 states, *"Mercy triumphs over judgment."* In the original language of the New Testament, the word *triumph* means "to boast in the face of judgment." Mercy is superior to anything deserving judgment. When the Lord extends mercy, He is saying, "My mercy prevails over the judgment you deserve." The Amplified Bible renders this verse, *"Mercy [full of glad confidence] exults victoriously over judgment."*

Throughout Scripture, men experienced God's power to restore and come back to their purpose. Jeremiah testified, *"Through the Lord's mercies we are not consumed, because His compassions fail not"* (Jeremiah 3:22). The word *consumed* means "to bring to a conclusion." In truth, a fall can bring an end to some of the most precious aspects of life, but mercy shields us until we come to our senses and turn back to God. God's mercy gives an opportunity for our lives never to conclude with failure because God's compassion never fails.

If a failure has set you aside, the desire to read this book is an indication that mercy is operating on your behalf. God will go to great lengths to bring you back to Him and back to your purpose in life. It's not over for you, even though you may feel that way at times. Because of His mercies, you have only begun to see the purpose of your life fulfilled.

FRESH MERCY EVERY DAY

Did you know that each rising sun is a fresh expression of God's love? His mercies appear with every break of dawn. Jeremiah says His mercies *"are new every morning"* (Lamentations 3:23). People may project a dismal forecast for you, but each sunrise is evidence

39

God has granted you favor to begin again. If you messed up yesterday, today is a new day, and you don't have to dread tomorrow. His mercy reappears to you *"every morning,"* which is why it cannot be measured. It just keeps showing up day-by-day.

Perhaps this is why it's impossible to know every time God has shown us His mercy. Imagine the times He sheltered us from casualties and harm without our being aware of it. I've wondered how many car accidents awaited me around the corner, but His mercy protected me. How many sicknesses have entered my body, but mercy caused the disease to pass through me unharmed? Through the years how many hardships did I face that would have otherwise buried me in a grave of despair? As I write to you, I write because of mercy.

Paul expressed it best to the church in Ephesus.

> *"But God, who is rich in mercy, because of His great love with which He loved us, even when we were dead in trespasses, made us alive together with Christ by grace you have been saved"* (Ephesians 2:4-5).

God is not close-fisted to withhold His storehouse of riches. From His abundant treasures He freely gives to us who are poor in spirit. Is it any wonder the psalmist repeatedly proclaimed, *"His mercy endures forever!"*

COMPASSION OVER YOUR RUINS

Have you wondered how God views your most repulsive falls and failures? After failing miserably, I often thought, "What does God think of me now?" I was aware of how some people viewed me after I failed and disappointed them. If God's opinion was anything like theirs, it wasn't good. I'm thankful even good people's opinions don't always reflect His. Devotion to God based on performance rather than intimate relationship often hides the goodness of God's restoring heart.

Possibly you've made bad choices that resulted in a disastrous outcome, or you were a victim of someone, and you reacted by walking away from God's designed path for your life. Perhaps family, friendships, career, church and even your faith have been shattered because something went awry. People, even people of faith, can be quick to offer their opinion about your circumstances. You know all too well how people view you, but do you know how God sees you? After all, what He thinks is what truly matters.

During a depressed era in Israel's history, Jerusalem became a burned-out city, and the Hebrew people scattered throughout Babylon as exiles. To that point, it was one of the lowest moments in the nation's history. The prophet Isaiah's words describe it as a time of *"desolation and destruction, famine and sword"* (Isaiah 53:19). Even so, God opens His heart to us who fall into these sad circumstances.

> *"The Lord will surely comfort Zion and will **look with compassion on all her ruins**; he will make her deserts like Eden, her wastelands like the garden of the Lord. Joy and gladness will be found in her, thanksgiving and the sound of singing"* (Isaiah 51:3, NIV, bold added).

When my life crashed, not a single trace of accomplishment was left to see. Hardly anything remained intact from my years of success and prosperity. My fall left me ruined.

Failure sometimes resembles a pile of ruins, just as the people Isaiah spoke about their situation. Even so, Isaiah boldly proclaimed the good news. *God does not look with disgust upon the ruins of our failures.*

Pause for a moment and take pleasure in knowing that when God looks at your worst disappointments, as He did with Jerusalem, He looks *"with compassion."* He tenderly observes each piece of your brokenness with mercy rather than judgment. When you are least aware of it, God is putting the pieces in place to rebuild your broken ruins. The prophetic declaration *"He will make her deserts like Eden, her wastelands like the garden of the Lord"* is what He's creating you to become. You see your ruins, but God sees a rebound.

Still, His mercy is not a quick remedy. Mercy holds us in God's embrace until He strengthens us to live in obedience. *"For a mere moment I have forsaken you, but with great mercies I will gather you. With a little wrath I hid My face from you for a moment; but with everlasting kindness I will have mercy on you"* (Isaiah 54:7-8). Mercy will carry us until He strengthens us to walk again and finally to one day run again.

Jack Deere once said, "Most of our problems arise from a misunderstanding of not realizing how much the Lord loves us." He does not love you more when you are doing well and less when you fail. Never make the mistake of interpreting the depth of His love from the vantage point of your successes or failures. The secret of King David's restoration was his revelation of God's lovingkindness after he murdered his military general and committed adultery with his wife.

BALANCING LOVE AND JUDGMENT

Paul gave the church at Rome the warning, *"Consider therefore the kindness and sternness of God"* (Romans 11:22). We do ourselves an injustice when we fall off either side of the fence of God's kindness and sternness. It's dangerous to consider the principles of life in Scripture as optional. As we rebound to life, intimacy with God and holiness of life are equally important.

Even so, God never "flies off at the handle," declaring, "I've had it up to here with you!" Even what we consider judgments, consequences of our falls, are expressions of mercy. He uses these difficult times to convince us that walking with Him is the way life is meant to be lived out.

GOD'S EXTREME LOVE AND KINDNESS

God looks for ways to lavish kindness upon broken people, because people are not always beautiful people. My wife calls individuals who appear to have a mistake-free life, "bubble people."

Who are these people? To us, they're people who look good and always appear to do the right thing. They seem to live in an unreal world of flawlessness, untouched by the issues the rest of us struggle with every day. Aside from dying of old age, nothing seems to happen out of the norm for those protected by the bubble. At one time I identified with bubble people. It was only after my bubble popped that I began to understand the extravagance of God's love for me. I'm still trying to comprehend the magnitude of it, and I always will, for His love is endless.

After the prophet Samuel anointed David as the king of Israel, the Lord displayed His heart to love the unlovely. A story in 2 Samuel reveals how Israel's new king wanted to honor his deceased friend, Jonathan, by showing kindness to someone in his family. David asked his servants, *"'Is there still anyone who is left of the house of Saul, that I may show him kindness for Jonathan's sake?'. . . And Ziba said to the king, 'There is still a son of Jonathan who is lame in his feet'"* (2 Samuel 9:1, 3).

Do you detect the same attitude in Ziba's voice that I do?

"Well, yes, your majesty," Ziba answers, "Jonathan did leave behind a son, but he's not quite like the rest of us. Well, you see, he has *this limp*. Honestly, your majesty, if you must know, *he's a cripple!*"

The boy's name was Mephibosheth. So David ordered that they bring him at once. They found him in the city of Lo Debar, which means "a dry place." It's common for those who have fallen and failed to live in dry places. It's the typical hangout for wounded victims of failure.

In ancient times a new king would often execute the remaining family members of the former monarch. They feared that someone from the previous royal family might challenge the newly crowned king for the throne. Can you imagine the concerns that entered Mephibosheth's mind as David's men approached him? He had been in hiding for years. In keeping with their customs, I'm sure he thought his end had come.

As the story unfolds, when *"Mephibosheth the son of Jonathan, the son of Saul, had come to David, he fell on his face and prostrated himself. Then David said, 'Mephibosheth?' And he answered, 'Here is your servant!'"* (2 Samuel 9:6). Mephibosheth could have tried to defend himself before the king on the basis that his father was his best friend. Instead, he humbled himself before King David. Once again humility will win the day.

David's response is a revelation of God's kindness you and I are invited to receive. *"So David said to him, 'Do not fear, for I will surely show you kindness for Jonathan your father's sake and will restore to you all the land of Saul your grandfather; and you shall eat bread at my table continually'"* (2 Samuel 9:7).

David not only showed mercy by refusing to kill him but also showered him with more than he could imagine. David restored all of his grandfather's land to him and gave Mephibosheth an honorary place in the royal family. Mephibosheth was invited to join King David and his family at the royal table for the rest of his life. When Mephibosheth pulled his crippled self up to the king's elegant table, David's provision of mercy covered his lifeless legs. Seated at the royal table, the limping Mephibosheth looked as normal as anyone else.

God wants to show you kindness too. Granted, you limp; but so did Jacob, so did Mephibosheth, and so did most of our heroes in the Bible. There is no rejection in mercy. God has filled His royal table with an abundance of compassion and lovingkindness, and His table has a seat only you can fill.

Chapter Five

Opening the Door of Repentance

Repentance is God's gift that invites us to leave where
we are and enter into the realm where He is.

The word *repent* often conjures up a religious image extracted
from nineteenth-century American revivalism. We picture a
preacher with a flush, contorted face and veins bulging from his
forehead. In one hand he holds a big black Bible and with the other
points his finger at his victims and screams, "Repent! Turn or burn!"
This approach may persuade a few people to "stop their sinning"
for a season, but it's usually short-lived. It is not the image the New
Testament word depicts and surely not the impression Jesus portrays.

The call to repent is the tender but persistent voice of the Holy
Spirit saying, "Your heavenly Father's kingdom has come, and He
longs for you to leave where you are and draw near to Him." The
conviction you feel is His pursuing love, appealing to you to reason
with Him (see Isaiah 1:18) about the direction you are choosing. The
unrest you sense is the Spirit Himself yearning for you to embrace
God's good future. The Holy Spirit even grieves over the potential
disaster of choices that miss the mark of God's best for you.

John the Baptist sets the stage for Jesus with the message
"Repent, for the kingdom of heaven is at hand" (Matthew 3:2).
John's message is the same one Jesus preached when He began His
ministry. The new thing God was doing not only came as a message
but as a new relationship. The Word would become flesh, touchable,

real, and be among people. Not only this, we would see God's glory as it's never before been seen (see John 1:14).

Jesus revealed His kingdom to a religious culture that related to God through a system of rules and law. If you kept the religious Law and associated with the right people group and religion, all was well. But if not, oh, well.

God's kingdom would challenge especially religious people to *rethink* God's character and how He relates to us. They were used to relating to God by obeying a religious protocol of rules and laws. The religious leaders taught that only those who did not stray from the letter of the Law stayed close to God.

Jesus showed up on the planet, healed any and everyone, ate meals in the homes of reprobates and touched lepers (considered in His day the most "unclean" of all people). With no previous religious training or pedigree, ordinary folk witnessed the glory of God while the Glorious One Himself lived within arm's reach of everyone.

Prostitutes, sinners and tax collectors loved spending time with Jesus. For the Jewish religious leaders, this was as scandalous as it could get. Why? Just this; their brand of religion taught that God was only favorable and merciful to those who did not break with their religious practice. What they witnessed was appalling and, according to their standards, disgraceful.

John and Jesus preached a message that resonated with religious outsiders. Their invitation to repent drew the masses which kindled jealousy in Pharisees and teachers of the Law. "Think again," John and Jesus contended, "about who God is to you and who you are to Him. He and His whole kingdom are as close to you as the reach of your hand." And so it was that even a Canaanite mother, pagans religiously, would receive divine healing for her daughter from Jesus. Her "pestering faith" pressed Him so far that He could not refuse her request, pagan or otherwise.

Unlike the Jewish Scriptures that had more than six hundred commands to keep, John and Jesus declared that only one condition stood between them and God's kingdom. They must repent. But what does that mean?

CHANGE THE WAY YOU THINK

The purest form of the biblical word for "repent" is the Greek word *metanoia*. It means "to change the way you think." Some define repent as "to turn around." Turning around, however, is the outcome and finale of repentance, and for most of us this is a process. But we will never change the direction we are taking until we first consider where the path we have taken is taking us.

The parable of the Prodigal Son in Luke's Gospel reveals that the boy turned to go back home after he *"came to his senses"* (Luke 15:17, NLT). Once he *rethought* how his actions had led him to the pigpen, he decided to return home to his father. He *reasoned* that even his father's hired servants at home were better off than he was in the pigpen. The New Testament understanding of repent means, *"Rethink where your choices are taking you; then come to God and accept the gift of His kingdom."*

John and Jesus did not compel people to repent to appease God's anger. Often, we hear a preacher urging people to turn from sin because God is displeased with their practice of evil. It's true He is not pleased when we practice lifestyles that lead us far away and out of touch with Him. His displeasure, however, is not from His anger *at us* but His love *for us*. He knows that a life lived outside His parameters of grace can, indeed, cause vital parts of our lives to die. His appeal for us to repent, however, is not a warning to turn *from something*, as much as it is an invitation to turn *to Someone*. Repentance is the gift God gives that leads from death in our world to life in His.

When the Holy Spirit convicts of sin, His conviction goes much deeper than just demanding we be good. He calls us to position ourselves to receive the Father's gift. It's impossible to hold on to wrong ways of thinking without those thoughts eventually becoming actions that take us down a path that leads to a "pigpen." Jesus Himself said, *"It is your Father's good pleasure to give you the kingdom"* (Luke 12:32). In love, the Holy Spirit bids us rethink our relationship with God and our position in life so we can receive all He has planned for us.

47

DECEPTION, CONCEPTION AND DEATH

Genuine repentance brings us face-to-face with the fact that we are conforming our life to patterns that are contrary to what God has planned. Paul cautioned, *"And do not be conformed to this world, but **be transformed by the renewing of your mind,** that you may prove what is that good and acceptable and perfect will of God"* (Romans 12:2, bold added). True repentance requires that we face the truth about ourselves. But it also calls us to face the truth about our God who is much more gracious than we ever thought Him to be.

A life lived outside of God's will can give the demonic realm legal access to our thoughts. The devil found an open door into Eve's life by appealing to her through *reasonable, rational thoughts.* As she processed the words of the serpent, she began to question God's good intention and purpose for their lives. In due course, distorted ideas and twisted rationale led her and Adam into disobedience and then their failure.

The enemy's schemes have not changed. Appealing to our minds through a myriad of avenues, he knows wrong thinking will lead to wrong actions that separate us from God and His purposes. Given the opportunity, the longstanding consequences of sin can blindside us. It begins as a small seed and progresses until it grows into an out-of-control tree. The New Testament letter of James describes this progression.

> *"But each one is tempted when he is drawn away by his own desires and enticed. Then, when desire has conceived, it gives birth to sin; and sin, when it is full-grown, brings forth death"* (James 1:14-15).

Sin begins with carnal desires in the heart fueled by thoughts conformed to this world. In the beginning these desires are mere "seed thoughts." Like all seeds, in the proper environment they are capable of growing and reproducing themselves. If we entertain these desires, they take root, conceive and produce (give birth) after their kind. We reap what we sow even in the thought realm. King Solomon, who reaped his own weedy garden in his later years, knew well how this process worked. He penned the often quoted prose of wisdom, *"For as he thinks in his heart, so is he"* (Proverbs 23:7).

GOD HAS A NEW HOME — AND IT'S YOU

I was a twenty-year-old, college-scholarship athlete when, for some strange reason, I decided to attend a gospel crusade at the football stadium of my college. Since I had been a successful athlete, football had become my "calling card." It was also my idol. All of this would change, however, after giving in to a friend who urged me to attend a church meeting called a "crusade" taking place on *my football field*. My friend guaranteed I would like the dynamic speaker. For some odd reason, I shined up my red MGB and put down the convertible top, and off I went, *alone*, to the crusade meeting.

Sitting with seven thousand other people, I had never heard anyone speak with such urgency and passion as this man. Evangelist James Robison preached a gospel I could understand. His fiery, forthright presentation about the second coming of Jesus impacted me so profoundly that it felt as if my insides literally quivered as he spoke. The few times I had attended church, I had never heard anyone speak of Jesus so convincingly. His passionate appeal captivated me. But it was the compassionate love I felt coming from this tall evangelist with wavy black hair that disarmed my pride and convinced me.

When he gave an invitation to receive Christ, with hundreds of others I wandered down the stadium steps (*my* stadium steps) and surrendered on the spot. On the fifty-yard line I laid down the idol all my friends knew me by and began following Jesus. On an August night in 1975 I asked Jesus Christ to forgive me of sin. It was the first time I had ever asked God to forgive me for anything, but it would not be the last.

I cannot logically explain what took place, but I know I was never again comfortable living the way I once did. Now understand, it was not that I could not sin or did not want to sin. Something in all of us, I think, has a bent to do what we should not do. Even Scripture acknowledges that sin can be pleasurable for a season (see Hebrews

11:25). It's just that I was no longer "at home" with it as I once was. The Holy Spirit did not simply change my behavior; He transformed my "internal atmosphere" and left me with an entirely new nature. I still feel sin tug on me at times, but it doesn't have the appeal it once had. The more I feed the nature of Jesus living within me, the less leverage sin has on me.

It was an incredible day when I finally understood Jesus did not die on the cross and rise from the dead to make me good. He suffered on the cross and rose from the grave *to make me His*. I no longer belonged to myself. God gave His Son and bought me out lock, stock and barrel (see 1 Corinthians 6:20). He wanted me as His home so much that He gave His best. He paid a high price for me—the life of His Son. Then by His Spirit He called me His home.

If you have come to Jesus and trusted Him to forgive your sin, you have the same testimony. God has a home, and that home is *you*.

Consequently, the Holy Spirit lets us know when we invite an outsider into His house. His grief over sharing His home with sin convicts us until we feel the misery of His sorrow. The Holy Spirit lets you know when trouble moves in because the Holy is not "at home" with the unholy.

> *"Do not grieve the Holy Spirit of God, by whom you were sealed for the day of redemption"* (Ephesians 4:30).

The uneasiness we feel is the Holy Spirit's voice communicating His sorrow calling us to repent—to think about—the thing that troubles Him. The Spirit knows if we accommodate the contrary thoughts we are likely to act upon them; then the seed is fertilized, reproduction begins, and, finally, something dies. Death manifests in various ways. Among those are family, marriage, relationships and countless virtues that define our purpose and destiny. He grieves, not because of a broken law, but more so because our actions will break us. His grief is one of love, not anger.

TAKING RESPONSIBILITY OPENS THE DOOR

Repentance is the front door, the first step, that leads us away from failure and back to the Father's purpose. We open this door by taking responsibility. Despite our choices, even if provoked by someone else's offense to us, being responsible opens the door from our prison into God's purpose.

Taking responsibility moves us from mere theory to practical steps back into relationship with God and into our purpose for which He called us. Everyone is invited to receive His kingdom, and everyone enters through the same doorway called repentance.

Years ago, while struggling with this, I called a friend and asked him to meet me for lunch. The choices I had made had left me lifeless. Many areas of my life were either dead or dying. The direction I took as a result of my poor thinking and choices affected my marriage, ministry and leadership position. Sin robbed me of self-esteem and confidence. More important, my relationship with God suffered.

Despite my hardship, I had a hard time owning responsibility for my part in my failure. As I related the story to my friend, I could not bring myself to call my sin by its ugly name. I was unaware of how deceived I was. I understood Scripture and certainly knew better, but I allowed deception into my thinking which had developed destructive patterns in my lifestyle. I referred to my failure as "a mistake" but could not bring myself to call my mistake by its disgusting name.

As only this friend could, he lovingly, but directly, quoted John 1:17, *"Grace and truth came through Jesus Christ."* With his piercing blue eyes staring at me, he said, "Bill, if you want the grace of God, you have to acknowledge the truth of God. You will never enjoy God's grace if you're not willing to acknowledge the truth. God is drawing near to help you. So just receive His grace and call your sin what it is."

*"**If we confess our sins**, He is faithful and just to forgive our sins and to cleanse us from all unrighteousness"* (1 John 1:9, bold added).

His words stung. Those words, however, were a turning point in my journey. Jesus had taken care of my sin two thousand years ago on the cross. But I would never enjoy the grace of His freedom until I was willing to take responsibility for my part and admit and confess it. When I did, the doorway swung open.

REFUSE TO PLAY THE BLAME GAME

Following Adam and Eve's fall, why did God look for Adam rather than Eve? It's because Adam carried the greater responsibility. After all, God told Adam, not Eve, from which tree to eat. Adam, however, responded by blaming Eve for his fall.

> *"The woman whom **You** gave to be with me, she gave*
> me of the tree, *and I ate"* (Genesis 3:12, bold added).

Beware of falling into the trap of the blame game as Adam did with Eve. It is the oldest trick of the devil, and given a chance our old nature will cuddle up to it. Blaming your actions on God or another person will hinder your rebound to walking in your purpose.

A typical response of someone playing the blame game sounds something like this: "I know what I did was wrong, but I wouldn't have done _____, had they not _____."

We fill in the blanks with legitimate and justified excuses, which highlights what someone else did or did not do to us.

We dare even to blame God. Some blame Him for not answering their prayer, so they throw fate to the wind and reason He doesn't care. The blame game justifies us and places the responsibility of our attitudes and actions upon someone else, even when that someone is God. In the long run, blame shifting our failure hardens our heart and postpones our return.

To Whom Should I Confess?

When the resurrected Christ charged the church in Ephesus to return to their first love, He instructed them to *"repent and **do** the first works"* (Revelation 2:5, bold added). Repentance is not feeling sorrowful or remorseful over your failure, but having the willingness to *do* whatever you should to set things right. Right actions should follow our change of mind and proper confessions. Our shift in thinking must have practicality. Otherwise, we risk going through motions, and our repentance is not entirely walked out. Repentance has to affect what we *do* as well as what we *believe*.

So the question arises, to *whom* should we confess? First, I suggest you take time to sit before God, allowing Him to work in your heart. The time you spend in His presence will be evident to people around you. Time in His presence humbles us and prepares us to do whatever He may ask us to do.

Second, depending on your role and responsibilities with others, a more public form of confession may be in order. Regarding this, Paul advised,

> *"Do not receive an accusation against an elder except from two or three witnesses. Those who are sinning rebuke in the presence of all, that the rest also may fear"* (1 Timothy 5:19-20).

The word *rebuke* means "to call into account." Repentance is made *"in the presence of all"* as a way to confess to those we are responsible for in some form of leadership. It could even be as small a circle as a father or mother before their children and family.

My hesitation and warning are for the church to take great care never to allow confession to shame people who admit to shortcomings that resulted in their fall. Shame never redeems or moves anyone from a fall and nearer to God. Shame is covered more extensively in chapter 11.

Admittedly, confessing our failure to anyone can be embarrassing. In an atmosphere of love and honor, when public repentance is in order, however, the result can be a beautiful lesson where everyone profits from someone else's mistakes. When such a noble spirit is present, rather than highlighting our frailty, we celebrate God's redeeming grace. After all, *"while we were still sinners, Christ died for us"* (Romans 5:8). It's our fallen nature that brought Jesus to earth and sent Him to the cross for us in the first place.

Confessing our failure is a process, and rarely a one-time act. Occasions to admit our faults evolve as we rebound to relationships and purpose. While you may make an initial confession, you should always be sensitive to the Holy Spirit when things come to mind that can lead you to further confession. Because our fall can affect so many people connected to our lives, the Lord is not only concerned with our freedom but also with those who were affected by our failure.

Because of my influence my fall affected people with whom I had no personal acquaintance. On one occasion I felt led to call a pastor in my city I had known for years. Since my failure became news in our little town I felt impressed to ask him to forgive me for wounding the body of Christ in our community. By this time, I had given up trying to protect my reputation, which had already become tainted. I wanted to be right before God, so I went to whomever I sensed I should ask to forgive me.

Six years later, after life had regained some normalcy, an act of my past resurfaced. By now, I considered myself relatively healed and rarely thought about the past. Nevertheless, one day while writing, words I had never thought of before came up in my spirit. "E-mail Jon and ask him to forgive you for lying to him." I knew precisely what the Holy Spirit was pointing out to me, though I had forgotten all about it. I stopped what I was doing and e-mailed him. He immediately replied, "I forgave you years ago. All is well, my friend."

God is gracious, revealing whom we should confess to as He knows we are ready and able to bear it. In fact, it's possible our emotions couldn't cope with the effects of our failure should He reveal all of the fallout at once. In His kindness God deals with us slowly and gently until we are ready to take the next step.

Don't be surprised after your pain subsides and life returns if the Holy Spirit deals with you about confessing to someone you've never considered. It may be He not only wants to deliver you at a deeper level but also free someone else who stumbled over your failure.

Drop the "If"

When you go to someone with a confession, eliminate *"if."* To approach someone and say, *"If* I have offended you, forgive me. . ." suggests, "I don't think I have offended you, but *if you think* I have, forgive me." Opening your confession with "if" merely cheapens it. When Pilate questioned Jesus, Scripture says, *"He answered him not one word"* (Matthew 27:14). Though blameless, Jesus offered no *ifs* in His defense. Likewise, lay aside your attempts to justify yourself with the opening line, *"If* I have offended you. . . ."

God Is Restoring All

In the book of Acts, Peter's Pentecost sermon begins the same way John the Baptist and Jesus started: *"Repent therefore"* (Acts 3:19). Then he adds, *"Until the times of restoration of all things"* (Acts 3:21). God plans to restore *"all things"* you lost from your failure. The rebound will be complete, but with conditions to walk out. Humbly, and yet confidently, enter the door of repentance. Repentance is the door that exits failure and the entryway that leads to God's purpose and destiny.

Chapter Six

Where Miracles Begin

Nothing in heaven or on earth has the capacity to transform the heart and heal the soul like a single act of forgiveness.

A teenager left home. At fifteen she would have never returned, but she was too young to make it on her own. Her behavior displayed her contempt for the values of her parents' upbringing. Now, running with the wrong crowd and dabbling in alcohol, marijuana and hard drugs, her personality changes were noticeable.

One night while with her friends she watched one of them overdose on heroin. He died in front of her as she witnessed the last glimmer of life leave his cold, gray body. Grief-stricken and scared, she returned home begging her parents to forgive her. They did. Returning to the God of her father and mother, she asked Him to forgive her too. This wayward teenager, now a young adult, serves as a missionary in India.

A husband and wife have become distant from one another. The sparkle of love left their marriage several years before he broke their marriage vows. For months he asked God to give him a plan to do whatever necessary to restore their marriage. One morning as he sat in silence he felt God draw abnormally near. God had come to answer his prayer, not with a plan but with His presence. God showed him, *Himself.*

In the light of God's loving yet convicting grace, this husband saw his wretchedness. More important, God allowed him to feel the pain of his wife's wounded heart. Feeling her broken heart broke him, and he began to weep violently. Composing himself and stumbling into their bedroom, the husband found his wife preparing herself for the day. When she saw him she thought he was in the midst of a heart attack. After convincing her he did not need to go to the hospital, he told her what happened. The remorse was real, God had broken him, and his wife saw his remorse was genuine. Over time, she was able to forgive him entirely, and the embers of love grew warm again.

Chapel services were a drag, but a regular part of a Christian college rooted in the Wesleyan holiness tradition. One wintry morning, chapel began as usual with a thousand students chattering away as they found a seat in the big ornate chapel. Instead of giving the typical sermon, the dean asked if any students wanted to give a testimony of their faith. The few who came forward didn't speak of their devotion, but their transgression. They confessed their need for forgiveness, for indiscretions that ranged from cheating and theft to prejudice and jealousy. Some approached classmates and teachers sitting in the pews to make restitution.

That chapel service lasted over a week, and the lights did not go out for 182 hours. Classes cancelled because students and professors were doing business with God and one another. The confessions of a few young people who needed forgiveness became the impetus of what became known as "The Asbury Revival of 1970."[2]

The stories above are real. Though the circumstances were vastly different, a common trait sparked a miracle in each situation. Forgiveness.

The most significant miracle of all begins the moment a person receives forgiveness of sin that Christ gave on the cross. The extraordinary power of forgiveness that changed us when we first received Him never loses its potency. Forgiveness is the place where miracles are born.

THE HIDDEN ROOT OF MANY VISIBLE PROBLEMS

Forgiveness has miracle-working properties that can heal the soul and alter a life's direction. Even healthcare professionals acknowledge that forgiveness has healing effects upon physical ailments and diseases. Perhaps more physical diseases and mental disorders than we are aware of can be traced to offenses rooted in unforgiveness. The need for forgiveness is the hidden root of many visible problems.

Jesus shocked everyone by publicly forgiving the sins of a paralytic man. Like many before him, the disabled man wanted Jesus to heal his legs. Instead, Jesus first healed his heart.

> *"Then behold, they brought to Him a paralytic lying on a bed. When Jesus saw their faith, He said to the paralytic, 'Son, be of good cheer; your sins are forgiven you'"* (Matthew 9:2).

Jesus had amassed a following that made religious leaders jealous. They were appalled when He pronounced the forgiveness of the paralytic man's sin. *"This man blasphemes!"* (Matthew 9:3) was their response when Jesus declared him forgiven for his sin.

Is it possible Jesus knew something they didn't? Perhaps the paralyzed man needed to be forgiven of sin *before* healing could come to his crippling condition. It's entirely possible the man's soul was more dysfunctional than his legs. Was the need for forgiveness the real prison that held him captive and crippled? It's only conjecture, but the possibility exists, and I believe it was, indeed, the base problem that kept him from walking.

> *"'Which is easier, to say, "Your sins are forgiven you," or to say, "Arise and walk"? But that you may know that the Son of Man has power on earth to forgive sins'—then He said to the paralytic, 'Arise, take up your bed, and go to your house.' And he arose and departed to his house"* (Matthew 9:5-7).

Jesus made a point. Certainly, it is easier to say, *"Your sins are forgiven,"* because forgiveness is a matter of the heart. We give and receive forgiveness by faith. Besides our testimony, we see no outward evidence that forgiveness has been granted or received. On the other hand, if physical healing comes after forgiveness is given or received, perhaps unforgiveness was, indeed, the root of the problem all along. We can't make a case by using this story alone because Jesus healed many people without first forgiving them. And yet that forgiveness can release healing to spirit, soul and body was witnessed in the Bible just as science confirms today.

THE KINGDOM IS LIKE FORGIVENESS

Jesus gave us the kingdom parables to describe how His world works. Since believers are citizens of His kingdom, it benefits us to live our lives with His world in mind.

In Matthew 18:23-35 Jesus revealed that life in His kingdom works by extravagant forgiveness. The parable describes a master who forgave a man of the ridiculous debt of ten thousand talents. In today's economy the amount remains in question, but some estimate the sum would equal millions of US dollars. Even with this immense debt against him, the master forgave him completely.

Once forgiven and free, Jesus says the forgiven man approached someone who owed him a mere one hundred denarii. At most, this came to a few thousand dollars (maybe less) in today's currency. Instead of showing his debtor the same mercy he had received from his master, he *"threw him into prison till he should pay the debt"* (Matthew 18:30).

When his cruel act was made known to the gracious master who had forgiven him the outrageous fortune he owed, the master called him a *"wicked servant"* (Matthew 18:32). The master then *"delivered him to the tormentors, till he should pay all that was due unto him"* (Matthew 18:34, KJV). The consequence of withholding forgiveness from the man who owed him such a slight amount was torment. It always is. If truth is known, the unforgiving person lives in a secret world of misery.

Over time, in one form or another, withholding forgiveness opens the door for tormentors. Whether these oppressors are mental, demonic or both, nonetheless, the result is always torturing. Sadly, time separates the offensive episode from the mental agony, and many never connect their miserable life to the forgiveness they withhold from the one who offended and hurt them. Withholding forgiveness can become an inroad for a demonic assault that leads so many people to resolve their problem in so many unfruitful places and ways. All along, the price of the miracle we need that can deliver everyone from anguish is as simple as forgiving someone from the debt they owe.

Forgiveness is one of the critical traits of God's kingdom. God sent His Son for this very purpose. *"In Him we have redemption through His blood, the forgiveness of sin"* (Ephesians 1:7). The outcome of Christ's forgiveness is so astounding that what He creates from the ashes of our failures are often more lovely than the life that existed before we failed. Once restored, the one forgiven no longer has to reflect on what "could have been." God's forgiveness reaches to the deepest levels of our spirits, and a transformation has taken place that is more beautiful than anything we could have imagined possible.

> *"If we confess our sins, He is faithful and just to forgive us our sins and to cleanse us from all unrighteousness"* (1 John 1:9).

Notice, John says, *"He is faithful."* Our faithfulness cannot determine our forgiveness. Forgiveness comes by the faithfulness of Jesus Christ. He is *"just,"* meaning His character is always consistent. He never wavers in His willingness to forgive us. To this day, Jesus lives to make intercession for us (Hebrews 7:25). Even after His death on the cross, He sits before God the Father interceding for us to say yes to His forgiveness and the new life He wants to give.

He doesn't regard people's evaluation of our sin. When we humble ourselves, He forgives sin with small or significant consequences. The promise is, *"If we confess our sins, He is faithful. . .to forgive our sins."* When we approach His throne of grace we have the assurance God will forgive us.

KING DAVID FOUND FORGIVENESS

King David is the classic example we turn to as someone who rebounded from multiple colossal failures. He is a historical and spiritual picture of God's grace. One writer noted that David's story is the Bible's epic display of a great God who forgives and restores the hideous falls of men. No other person in the Bible gives hope to those of us who have failed, as does David.

David's known offense is adultery and murder, in that order. When the prophet Nathan confronted him with his sin, he didn't flinch but immediately confessed his transgression. Without excuse, he humbled himself and admitted, *"I have sinned against the Lord"* (2 Samuel 12:13). Psalm 51 is David's prayer and emotional appeal that will forever brand him as the confessed fallen king. This worshipping military giant fell hard with adultery and murder on his account. Even so, a thousand years after his death, David was still known as a man after God's heart (see Acts 13:22).

How could David bring himself to repent so completely? I suggest he risked everything because of his previous encounters with God. David had experienced God's presence and character and knew Him to be loving and merciful. Instead of running away in fear, he knew he could run to Him and be received.

David didn't rationalize his failure. He was willing to be known for what he was, Israel's fallen king. Admitting his murder, David wrote, *"Deliver me from bloodshed, O God"* (Psalm 51:14). His fame as a king and military leader was so widespread there's little doubt he could have escaped the problem he created had he wanted to do so. He could have found people to lie and cover for him. But David's experience with God ran deeper. So he bowed low, taking the high road, confessing the cause of his fall.

King David prayed a prayer no one else under Old Covenant Law dared or attempted to pray. In truth, no one else could have prayed such a prayer because no one else knew God in the way David did.

> *"Have mercy upon me, O God, according to Your lovingkindness; according to the multitude of Your tender mercies, blot out my transgressions. Wash me thoroughly from my iniquity, and cleanse me from my sin"* (Psalm 51:1-2).

Lovingkindness. Here's a word that's close kin to our New Testament word *grace*. His intimate encounters with God gave David a revelation of grace long before a covenant of grace existed. As he poured out his confession of sin to God, he knew that, according to the Law of Moses, he did not have a leg to stand on. Even Israel's king had no defense under the Law. The Law required them to stone to death anyone with an offense of David's nature.

David, however, appealed to the One he had intimately worshipped and met face-to-face in the secret place. He approached God and made his appeal for mercy and grace, something the average Hebrew born under the Law would not have conceived doing. No one approached Jehovah in this manner. But as David had done so many times before, the sweet singer of Israel strummed the heartstrings of God and was forgiven.

As soon as David confessed his sin before the prophet, his answer came, *"The Lord also has put away your sin; you shall not die"* (2 Samuel 12:13). He was restored from his fall back to intimacy with his God because David knew God to be a God of *lovingkindness*.

This same lovingkindness is there for you. The revelation David knew is made known through the Lord Jesus Christ. *"But God demonstrates His own love toward us, in that while we were still sinners, Christ died for us"* (Romans 5:8). This verse is not only valid for those coming to Christ the first time but applies to us every time we need forgiveness. The love of God is demonstrated through Christ each time we embrace His sacrifice on the cross.

FORGIVENESS IS SUMMED UP IN C.H.R.I.S.T

Most people, believers included, are unaware of how much they rely on their performance to justify who they are in Christ. We are prone to try to earn our way through our good behavior. It's difficult to switch from performing *for* God to just *believing* Him. We often assure others of the riches of Christ's mercy, but when we are in need, often we have difficulty receiving His forgiveness ourselves.

Forgiveness is not complicated. In its fullness, forgiveness is summed up in Christ. Allow me to outline it this way.

C. Forgiveness Is a Choice

In receiving God's forgiveness or in forgiving someone else, it is a choice. You choose to accept the forgiveness Christ has already given to you. You can do nothing to repay for failing Him. Assuming it was a sin that caused your failure, if you choose to remain in it the fallout will continue. On the other hand, after asking God to forgive you, not receiving His gift of forgiveness is unbelief. Simply giving thanks to God for His forgiveness is the beginning of putting your faith in motion to believe and accept His gift.

Forgiving others who have offended and hurt you is also a choice. Perhaps they violated your trust or rejected your efforts to amend your errors. Forgiving them is not something you feel, but a hard decision you make. Recall the account I mentioned above from Matthew 18:23-35. The Lord called the man who refused to forgive *"wicked"* (Matthew 18:32). Receiving and giving forgiveness begin with a choice you make.

H. Forgiveness Is from the Heart

Understanding God sent His Son who lived among us, died on the cross for our sins and rose from the grave can become a cold intellectual fact. Knowing facts about God will not change us. Believing Him with the heart does.

Paul said it this way, *"For **with the heart one believes** unto righteousness, and with the mouth confession is made unto salvation"* (Romans 10:10, bold added). He encouraged us to confess with our mouth what we say we believe in our heart. At the top of our confession should be His unconditional love and His willingness to forgive. As we speak and hear the truth of His love and forgiveness, our heart's capacity expands and becomes transformed by His truth and grace.

R. Forgiveness Brings Righteousness

Some of you, I am sure, understand by experience the Scripture that says, *"All our righteous acts are like filthy rags"* (Isaiah 64:6, NIV). On your most brilliant day you are aware of how badly you miss the mark. Now that you have come to grips with the severity of your failure, you're ready to replace your ruins with His righteousness.

Looking again at the story of the wayward son, leaving his father's house to journey into sin, the boy *"came to his senses"* (Luke 15:17, NLT) and decided to return home. On the way back, we find him rehearsing the speech he plans to give to his father.

> *"I will arise and go to my father, and will say to him, 'Father, I have sinned against heaven and before you, and I am no longer worthy to be called your son. Make me like one of your hired servants'"* (Luke 15:18-19).

When the boy comes face-to-face with his father, he starts to rattle off the words he practiced on the way home. Before he can repeat his memorized spiel, his dad interrupts, ordering his servants, *"Bring out the best robe and put it on him"* (Luke 15:22). This robe represents a robe of righteousness (Isaiah 62:10, Revelation 6:11), hardly what one would think the lad deserves. The moment God sees a returning son or daughter a divine exchange takes place. We give Him our old lives filled with the stench of the pigpen, and He gives us His royal robe of righteousness that covers the evidence of our past and the lingering smell we still bear.

I. Forgiveness Is Intercession

Jesus *"always lives to make intercession"* (Hebrews 7:25) for you. No matter what you have done or where you stand, His position for you never changes. He stands before His Father on your behalf.

Even now, Christ's act of mercy on the cross is eternally satisfying to the Father. He is always for you.

Moses stood between Israel and God as an act of intercession for God's people (Exodus 32). They had sinned, and the Lord released His wrath against them to the degree that He told Moses He would destroy them and start over with him. Moses would not hear of it. Standing between God and the Israelites, *"Moses pleaded with the Lord his God"* (Exodus 32:11). Moses' capacity to forgive Israel of their waywardness became an act of intercession before God. If Moses, a man with a murder record, could stand before God and change the destiny of a nation, how much more efficient is Jesus Christ's intercession for you?

S. Forgiveness Is Salvation

God's forgiveness is so transforming that Scripture calls the forgiven a *"new creation"* (2 Corinthians 5:17). A simple plea for forgiveness so stirs the heart of God that He gives grace so the person crying out to Him becomes a whole new race of people.

I'm thankful this grace never ceases at any point in our lives. Dr. Jimmy May, one of my theology professors at Emory University, would proudly proclaim in his lectures, "I was saved, I am being saved, and I shall be saved!" Dr. May discovered his salvation did not come at a point in history but was an ongoing, daily experience that began at the cross and would continue until he stood before the throne of God.

Have you noticed the power of those two little words, "Forgive me"? At the humble admission of an offense and the request for forgiveness, walls that divide people fall, and relationships heal. Your salvation began, continues and will come to its full purpose each time God hears you pray, "Forgive me."

T. Forgiveness Transcends Our Ability

Forgiveness is God's supernatural grace that transforms us into Christ's image in the same way unforgiveness can entrench us in our own. By humbly receiving God's forgiveness we transcend our human ability to forgive others. When we grasp the vast love of God's forgiveness to us, He enables us to forgive others beyond our natural capabilities. While observing his patients in the mental ward of a hospital, a psychiatrist testified, "At least half of these people would walk out of here tomorrow if only they knew they were forgiven." Forgiveness is the divine ability of God to transform the human spirit.

Many people would experience freedom if they believed what the Lord says about them. *"If we confess our sins, He is faithful and just to forgive us our sins and to cleanse us from all unrighteousness"* (1 John 1:9). Our little pea brains cannot comprehend how it's possible to abolish our past. I repeat what I said earlier, that transformation is possible on the basis that *"He is faithful,"* not because we are faithful. When we receive God's faithfulness to forgive, we become more willing to risk forgiving others who have sinned against us.

FORGIVING YOURSELF

Forgiving ourselves can be a challenge. If this is the case with you, here's some advice. *Stop playing God.*

When we don't forgive ourselves, we put ourselves in place of God. My goal has been to highlight that God forgave us by sacrificing His own Son for our complete freedom. When we read the story of Christ's love on the cross, we conclude that God is a forgiving and loving God. Love and forgiveness are not something He does; *it's who He is. "God is love"* (1 John 4:16).

If God's Word declares He forgives you, isn't something off-center when you will not forgive yourself? Are your standards higher than His? Are your ways higher than His ways? Do you think that, given time, you can earn the right to be forgiven by almighty God? This performance thinking is a trap that will ensnare you to the past. You will never enter into your destiny by remaining tethered to your history.

When God rebounds our lives, we learn to trust Him completely, believing He is as faithful and kind as the Bible says He is. Jesus has already unlocked the door that incarcerated you, so stop playing God. Believe Him, forgive yourself and walk out of your prison.

WHEN PEOPLE DO NOT FORGIVE

Disappointment is usually at the root of people's choice to keep us in their prison of unforgiveness. They express their frustration by rejecting us. Others, while saying they forgive, may not want us to forget how we hurt them when we failed. Knowing people hold your past against you is difficult to cope with when you're doing all you know to do to move forward.

What's the key to being free from their rejection? *Forgive them for not forgiving you.* Forgiving people when they refuse to forgive you releases God's grace. After all, undeserved forgiveness is at the core of the gospel. I've seen this principle work in my life. It caused broken relationships to reemerge, sometimes immediately, and other times, years down the road. If you have people who want to live in your history, let them; but don't you for a minute think you have to live there with them. You cannot walk into your destiny if you don't let go of your history. Surround yourself with people who choose to define you by your purpose rather than your past.

FORGIVENESS AND RESTORATION

If repentance is the doorway to restoration, forgiveness is the first room in the house. It's the place where miracles begin. Forgiveness is the balm that stops the bleeding and allows healing to begin its work.

On the other hand, forgiveness is not the same as being fully restored. We make a mistake if we suppose God's forgiveness and our rebound are the same things. God forgives the moment we confess it to Him. Rebounding, however, is a process. And you will find that being restored to people takes more time than restoration to God. That's because God is perfect, and we are not. We humans process a crisis over time. We need time to accept, forgive and enjoy a restored relationship.

Forgiveness sets the miracle in motion. And while it's only the beginning, it's enough to encourage you to keep pursuing God and the destiny He assigned to you.

Chapter Seven

Ditch Dwellers, Samaritans and Relationships

Moses raised a shepherd's rod over the Red Sea, and God pushed back the waters. Elisha lay prostrate upon the corpse of the Shunammite woman's son, and God raised him from the dead. A lame beggar sat at the temple gate for years; then Peter prayed, and he started jumping, leaping and praising God. Surely God does not need a mortal man to help Him work miracles, but sometimes we do.

"You don't need to be driving. There are still icy spots on the roads, and you don't know they're there till it's too late. And besides, if you end up in a ditch somewhere, I'm not going to be home today to pull you out."

That was my dad's warning. I rolled my eyes thinking as I had before that he was overreacting. After all, I was sixteen and had been driving for six months with no problems.

We had had a big snowfall the night before, at least five inches or more. Where we live in the South, that's big. The thing about snow in the South—it comes, and it goes. Roads that are snow packed and icy in the morning can be clear and bone-dry by late afternoon.

In a few minutes my dad left, and so did I. Because of the snow the schools stayed closed (another perk of snow in the South), so my friends and I planned to meet at the junior high gym to play some basketball. After the game with the guys I decided to take a shortcut home down a winding country road. With my eight-track player belting out Grand Funk Railroad's "Are You Ready?" I put my '67 Chevelle "in the wind" and headed home. Looking back, I was not at all ready for what lay ahead.

When I rounded a curve, a solid sheet of white icy snow covered the road! For about an eighth of a mile, tall pines shaded both sides and kept the sun from touching that stretch of highway. I hit my brakes (big mistake), and my car began to spin around like a ballerina. In seconds I saw north, south, east and west until my vehicle slid into an icy ditch.

The only thing that was hurt was my ego. I pushed open the door and trekked up a snowy bank to a house beside the road. Cell phones did not exist in those days, so I used their phone to call Dad at work. After I told him what happened, he came to my rescue, and with his truck and a chain pulled my car out of a trench about three feet deep. Dad didn't scold me or say, "I told you so." He knew I knew what I did was stupid. Now his part was to help me out of my predicament, not remind me of my failure.

Dad's warning came from experience. So does God's. Like my day in the ditch, we don't always heed God's warnings the first time. Instead, we assume we can live fast, take shortcuts and reach our destination. Then we run upon an unexpected slippery road and end up in a ditch. As my life unfolded, I discovered this was not the last time I would have to depend on someone to help pull me out of trouble.

LIFTING THE FALLEN OUT OF THE DITCH

In chapter 10 of Luke's Gospel, Jesus provoked the religious leaders by telling a parable about a man who *"fell among thieves. . .leaving him half dead"* (Luke 10:30). It's traditionally known as the parable of the Good Samaritan, but it's more accurately the parable about the man in the ditch. The focus of the story is the man who fell and was left half dead. The question was, "Who would pick him up?" Getting up would require someone to come alongside to help him get back up and heal. Jesus' concern was for the fallen, wounded man.

Before we tackle the question of who would help him, it's essential we know what Jesus did not ask. Often, religious circles decide whether a *"half-dead"* ditch-dweller is worthy of being lifted up based on how and why he fell in the first place.

Jesus never imposed the question as to why the man chose a route that was a known hiding place for thieves. Few people traveled the road from Jerusalem to Jericho without being robbed. Who was this guy to think he was the exception and would escape the consequences others did not? We can ask ourselves the same question. How did we think we could do what we did and avoid the fallout? It's not that we should not address the issue, for, indeed, we should. But, oddly enough, Jesus never entertained the question about the man in this parable. His sole focus was on lifting him up from his fall.

The first people to come upon him were religious leaders. A priest walked by, and then a Levite, and both ignored the half-dead man in the ditch. Perhaps they were ashamed to be associated with him, but more likely they didn't respond because their religious law forbade them from touching such a man. They were taught not to associate with him.

Before we're quick to judge, let's give the religious leaders the benefit of the doubt. It's entirely possible these men did not know how to respond or what to do for a man in this position. If this was their reason for passing by, I can feel their pain of awkwardness.

At one time I felt a similar uneasiness when approached by a homeless person. Since I couldn't relate to him, I pretended I didn't see him. He became invisible to me. I did not feel superior; I was merely uncomfortable because I could not relate to the pain of his brokenness. So, like the priest and the Levite, I turned my eyes in the other direction and walked on, leaving him where he was.

Unless you've been there, it's difficult to understand how good people can end up in the ditches of life, wounded by the consequences of their actions. Adding to the uneasiness, if it's someone you know, and you've never seen them in this condition, it makes approaching them even more embarrassing.

Jesus was as much a "son of man" as He was the "Son of God." He was God, living with us as one of us, experiencing the lure of sin as we do. Hebrews 4:15 states, *"For we have not a high priest which cannot be touched with the feeling of our infirmities; but was in all points tempted like as we are, yet without sin"* (KJV). He never sinned, but He knows how we feel because He felt the pull of sin upon His life. Jesus knows the feelings of failure merely from experiencing the lure of temptation. We should use the same compassion when we approach anyone who has suffered a fall. Even if we've never traveled their Jericho Road, our own nature can help us understand the pain they feel.

It is a known fact that Jews blatantly rejected Samaritans. It's no surprise a commonly rejected Samaritan would become the hero of this story. The one who understands rejection stops to pick up this wounded and refused soul. His compassionate response was to place the injured man in an environment where he could heal. Not only this, he promised to pay his debt until he fully recovered. What a likeness of the Lord Jesus Himself!

Rarely, if ever, does anyone rebound alone. God's kingdom is relational, and He uses people, often people you would least expect, to help you up out of your ditch. The people you once rejected may be the individuals who are compassionate enough to raise you up out of the gutter. Usually they are the ones who understand the pain you are experiencing. From now on, you too will know when you see others lying lifeless on the side of life's road. Next time the Samaritan someone leans on could be you.

LEANING, LOVE AND ACCOUNTABILITY

I suppose nothing bears fruit in God's kingdom like relationships based on mutual love and respect. Love is the foundation of real accountability. Love-based relationships empower us to live our God ordained-purpose while walking in love with those around us. In these types of relationships, both encouragement and correction are well received.

I don't like what accountability has come to mean in some circles. Why? It suggests it is a patrolling system where keepers-of-the-law make sure its constituents stay in line and don't break any rules. At worst, it represents a "sin patrol" standing guard over potential law-breakers. Authentic accountability is entirely different. It's a heart-to-heart relationship of trust with love as a mutual bond.

I've heard too many stories from Christians with a significant failure in their lives whose church or denomination assigned a mentor to oversee their progress. They were to report to the mentor, by phone or in person. Here's the problem. It's doubtful that "half dead" people, lying in the ditch, will risk the pain in their lives with someone who has been "assigned" to them. Such a relationship often positions itself on fulfilling the organization's policy, rather than genuine rapport between two people.

We've already mentioned how God's husband-and-wife team, Adam and Eve, was the most profound accountability partnership God would create. Their love for one another not only fulfilled intimacy but was also to protect and inspire each other's destiny.

Moses had his father-in-law, Jethro. After seeing Moses struggling with the daily problems from thousands of Israelites, Jethro showed Moses a more practical way to serve the people.

David had a similar relationship with the prophet Nathan. Their relationship was so heartfelt that Nathan never doubted whether or not David would receive him. Nathan's confrontation saved the king and a nation.

Elisha had Elijah. The two lived in such close communion that Elisha would not separate himself from his spiritual father, though Elijah charged him to go home. It's sad when our concept of accountability portrays a guardrail to only correct us rather than a stairway to take us higher.

The word *accountability* reveals its significance. Grounded in authentic relationships, it should lead us to give an *account* to one another for the gifts and callings God has placed within us. Our *ability* then increases as the give-and-take of relationship takes place. This kind of accountability provides a flow of life between people that encourages growth.

No one is so strong to live independently of others, much less independently from God. God said to Adam, *"It is not good that man should be alone"* (Genesis 2:18). This statement was not addressing loneliness, but a relationship that would help him live out his divine purpose on earth.

As a high school and college athlete, I discovered our team could not excel without a coach. More than a teacher, the coach kept us focused on the task of playing to win. Today, coaching has become commonplace in every discipline of life. From business to basketball, you can hire a coach to make you better. What we're doing when we hire a coach is obtaining a relationship with someone who will keep us accountable to develop our gifts and become our best at fulfilling a goal.

You were not created to do life alone, and you will never be your best if you isolate yourself from others. God encourages relationships, not only to help you rebound out of a ditch but also to impart gifts and abilities that exceed your limitations.

WHY WE AVOID ACCOUNTABLE RELATIONSHIPS

Affirming relationships help us live out the potential God put within us and strengthen us in every area of life. So why do we shun these relationships?

First, we fear rejection. Some of the strongest, most capable people fear mutual submission where they share an honest and authentic connection. At times, a strong personality is evidence of fear and insecurity, rather than strength and authority. A stable and resilient inner man is where our greatest strength lies, and this requires vulnerability.

Going through life without being rejected at some level is impossible. In my quest to find someone to help me come back from failure, I made an appointment with a leader of a vital, international ministry. I risked spilling my guts and sharing my complicated story. At the end of our time, I asked if he would agree to meet with me occasionally. He replied that he would "pray about it."

A week later I received a phone call from him, and to my surprise he said, "The Lord doesn't want me to meet with you." Another rejection. Fortunately, by this time I knew it was God's will to restore me, so I determined to trust Him to bring relationships into my life who would help me along the way. And He did.

Second, we avoid accountability because trusting relationships take time to develop. Time is precious and fleeting. We rarely give our time until emergencies force us. When I realized I needed this kind of relationship, I asked God to send them into my life. I prayed for men I could trust, and yet who would speak truth into my life.

One of my most meaningful experiences came when a mutual friend introduced me to a Christian leader. Over time, relationship and trust developed between us until I told him my story. Nothing I said shocked him. After hearing me out, he never estranged himself from me but was also aware I had not completely healed. Furthermore, he sensed I struggled to forgive myself.

At this stage, I developed an emotional need to be excessively transparent with people I met. Early on in a new friendship I would find ways to allude to my failure, only because I feared my new acquaintance would hear about my past through the grapevine. This kind of transparency can be harmful, which I'll explain later.

While attending a seminar at his church, he walked over to me and said, "Bill, the Lord wants you to know He's okay if you never say anything else about what happened." He then walked away and never referred to his statement again. It proved to be a prophetic moment. Taking his advice set me free from feeling the need to bare my story to every new acquaintance I made.

Third, we run from accountability because people are not always trustworthy and loyal. It's still not wise to be transparent with everyone. Not everyone has the strength of character to bear the burden of your inner struggles and failures. In fact, not everyone is supposed to shoulder this load. Seeking sympathy can be dangerous.

Ted Haggard related to me the story of him and two friends on an overseas ministry trip many years ago. Weary from their flight, they decided to stay through the day in a hotel, rest up and spend some time in prayer in preparation for their ministry. In an atmosphere of prayer and mutual accountability, they became transparent, sharing personal vulnerabilities and weaknesses. Together, they agreed to pray and support one another to live Christ-like lives. It was genuine spiritual accountability among brothers in Christ, or so it seemed.

Ten years later, now in the agony of scandal, Ted discovered that one of the men he prayed with on that ministry trip chose to go public with personal information he confided while praying with him. It's possible this individual thought, as many do, that the world needs to know the truth. Since Ted was now a well-known leader throughout the body of Christ, it's also likely personal notoriety could have been the real motive for disclosing Ted's private struggle he shared in prayer ten years earlier.

Choose your confidants prayerfully. What you share in mutual accountability today could be used against you later, should life circumstances change. Genuine relationships surface during difficult seasons in life when friendship with you becomes risky. Given to the wrong person, the information you unveil today could injure you tomorrow. Use wisdom with those you invite into your inner circle. Even with risks, God uses relationships with the right people to heal our wounds and lift us to the potential He has placed within us.

AUTHENTIC ACCOUNTABILITY

Genuine accountability is not born out of a spirit to reprimand the offender, but from a heart that anticipates his rise from a fall.

> *"Two are better than one, because they have a good return for their work: If one falls down, **his friend** can help him up. But pity the man who falls and has no one to help him up!"* (Ecclesiastes 4:9-10, NIV, bold added)

Solomon insists it's a *"friend"* who helps us up when we fall. Notice the goal is to *"help him up"* rather than merely keep his sin in check. If this relationship only manages behavior, no change at the heart level will take place.

When rebounding from failure is only a program to fulfill, it's doubtful that going through the program will heal us. Rebounds require rebounders. On the basketball court the center position is the person who places himself in the middle of the fight and contends for the rebound to keep the ball in play. Usually the tallest man on the team, he has a perspective and advantage no one else has. We need someone with a better view, who will stand in the middle, contending with and for us.

Consider Jesus Christ who was unashamed to be *"numbered with the transgressors"* (Luke 22:37). In a spirit of humility, Jesus came to fallen humanity to restore us to God. He was willing to be *"numbered"* among us, identifying with us, as one of us. The New Living Translation renders the verse, *"He was counted among the rebels."* Jesus was willing to become like us in the flesh, identifying with us as rebellious failures, to restore us. Jesus stands in the middle of our fight and grabs the rebound that keeps us in the game.

The willingness to mix with the unlovely is the attitude God uses to lift up the fallen. Jesus was not ashamed to be identified with sinful humanity, and neither should we. Accountability that restores walks humbly beside the failures of life until they return to where they were before their fall. And these are the ones who help others become better than they were before they fell.

We are most vulnerable to cynicism and cold-heartedness after a failure. It's not uncommon to want to quit everything and everyone, including our devotion to God. In these seasons, you don't have to be the life of the party, but neither should you isolate yourself. Take advantage of corporate gatherings with other believers. Ride upon the wings of the worship of others, soaking in God's presence as they worship Him.

While driving to a church service, I recall how I dreaded seeing a swarm of smiling faces. I would counter them with a polite plastic smile. As the worship began, however, I sensed my heart grow warm as I sat among others worshipping God. After a while, I could feel His presence again. I had nothing to offer; I merely rode on their wave of worship into His presence and began to feel Him heal my soul. At the time, I couldn't rise and touch God alone, but as others worshipped around me I did.

*"If two lie down together, they will keep warm.
But how can one keep warm alone?"* (Ecclesiastes
4:11, NIV).

Getting up from your fall and failure is far more than rees-
tablishing your reputation before people. God is restoring you to
Himself. Whatever the cause when you fell, more than your reputation suffered. There was a significant blow to your heart and
soul. In failure we feel that we have lost something. These losses
can cause our heart to grow cold. Relationships with other people
walking with God help us *"keep warm"* toward Him and life in
general. Otherwise, we isolate ourselves, which endangers our love
growing cold.

It doesn't take a lot of pressure to break us. A person walking
alone will find it easier to surrender to various kinds of stress. It takes
courage to step out of a pit, and especially one when you refused to
pay attention to the warning. A brother or sister by your side can
impart courage and hope as you walk through this harsh emotional
terrain. If you are sincere about rebounding to God and your purpose, you can be sure God will send someone to help you out.

SUBMISSION TO OTHERS

As long as you remain in isolation, fear will keep you hidden.
You will find freedom, however, when you bring your darkness into
the light. When you come into the light with a trusting relationship,
God's beauty shines upon the concealed darkness. Once in the light,
it severs the leverage the enemy used against you. In the presence
of light darkness ceases to be. John describes it this way: *"But if we
walk in the light as He is in the light, we have fellowship with one
another, and the blood of Jesus Christ His Son cleanses us from all
sin"* (1 John 1:7).

Each case is different, and the time frame to rebound will vary
depending upon the nature of the offense and the condition of the
heart. The depth of our recovery does not depend upon the strength
of a program but on the humility of heart from the one getting up.

It's my prayer when we find a brother or sister in a ditch we will treat each as Jesus would, with tender, individual care.

THE NEED FOR WISE COUNSEL

The offense that caused us to fail is most often the fruit rather than the root of the problem. There may be a need for prolonged counseling with a Spirit-led counselor who can spot the source of the issue and bring healing. In many cases, failures come from a crisis or trauma buried in the past. Freedom from these types of issues usually requires professionals who are trained and anointed for the task.

A licensed, professional counselor can also be a safe haven. The licensed counselor, held liable by law, is forbidden to share information you disclose to them. They may satisfy any fears you have regarding whether or not they would be unfaithful with your personal information.

A level of supernatural healing is available through Holy Spirit-led believers. A prophetic ministry gift of loving deliverance can help heal deep-rooted wounds. When someone needs more profound emotional and spiritual healing, I recommend someone trained in a ministry of loving counsel and deliverance. If the person (or people) walking alongside you recognizes your need for more in-depth healing, listen to them. Most likely, their insights are on target. To reject them could not only prolong your recovery but be a short-term fix making you vulnerable to another fall.

PUBLIC LIFE AND ACCOUNTABILITY

Keep in mind that you may not be the only one bearing wounds from your failure. Relationships in your sphere of influence may also be suffering from your actions. Knowing you have willingly submitted yourself for healing can release healing to their lives as well. Subjecting yourself to counsel testifies that you are not making light of your failure and speaks well of your attempt to rebuild character and integrity. You gain respect by being responsible for your part in it. You will often have more respect afterward than you had before your failure because your confession is an outward recognition of your stand for truth.

Concerning Jesus, Scripture says, *"Though He was a Son, yet He learned obedience by the things which He suffered"* (Hebrews 5:8). Though He was sinless, through submission Jesus *"learned obedience."* All the more, should we not *"learn obedience"* by willingly submitting ourselves to relationships that direct and encourage us to rebound to fulfill our purpose and destiny.

Chapter Eight

For the Love of Discipline

A winding, bumpy road called "The Way of Discipline" stretches from our past into our future. It's sparsely traveled because the way is often dismal, and at times the destination seems unreachable. Only the daring will attempt this journey, for this is where God molds us into the person we knew He created us to be all along.

Years ago, my friend Jon accepted a position as the general manager of a radio station in a beach town in Florida. After his family settled into their new home, he and his wife invited me to spend some time with them.

Now let me explain what was involved in spending time with them. In those days they had six children. They were wonderful children, mind you, but they were children. Not exactly the setting I usually choose as a getaway for peace and quiet. But I needed time away and wanted to visit my friend, so I headed south.

Twenty-five years later, my week with Jon and his family still has a prominent place in my memory. During my visit, I remember their children doing all the things children do. They played, laughed and whimpered a bit. What caught my attention, however, was how they worshipped, prayed and respected adults. I witnessed Jon and his wife's consistency of discipline and how they did it with such love. Even more, I've seen the fruit of their parenting as they prepared each child to fulfill his or her distinct destiny.

In case you wonder, their kids didn't go through the day like robots for fear their parents might whack them if they did not perform up to expectations. They lived like normal kids, but it was the best normal anyone could imagine. I never anticipated being so refreshed after spending a week in the same house with six children.

As we said our goodbyes, I told Jon and his wife, "You're so good at this; you should have six more kids!" As it turned out, they did, in fact, have two more children, eight total. At this writing, all but one are grown and out of the house. Their life's work includes missionaries to other nations, inner-city ministries, a graphic-computer technician, church planters, church musicians, worship leaders and a youth pastor, just to name a few. Most important, they're all serving the Lord.

Through the years I've learned something unique about discipline, and in particular God's discipline. *He does not discipline us to keep us in line, but to keep us on track.* He allows us to simmer in our circumstances, for it's the stuff we face day-in-and-day-out that prepares us for our destiny. Solomon wrote, *"Train up a child in the way **he should go"** (Proverbs 22:6, bold added). Notice it does not say in the way he should *behave*. God is not paranoid that our behavior might be an embarrassment to Him. He does discipline us, however, so that negative patterns don't short-circuit our future purpose. *Discipline is the process God uses to prepare us for our next mission, rather than punish us for our past mistakes.*

In the last chapter we saw how relationships are vital to a lifestyle of connection and accountability. Discipline takes us a step further to strengthen our character, so we're equipped to bear the weightiness of our mission. It helps to recognize that the word *discipline* is both a noun and a verb. Discipline is a process as well as a product; a journey as well as a destination. Discipline—the process—creates disciples—the product. Discipline strengthens character and puts us on a track in life that takes us in a direction where we can fulfill our God-given destiny.

The Magna Carta of God's discipline is found in Hebrews 12:5-13.

"And you have forgotten that word of encouragement that addresses you as sons: 'My son, do not make light of the Lord's discipline, and do not lose heart when He rebukes you, because the Lord disciplines those He loves, and He punishes everyone He accepts as a son.'

"Endure hardship as discipline; God is treating you as sons. For what son is not disciplined by his father? If you are not disciplined (and everyone undergoes discipline), then you are illegitimate children and not true sons.

"Moreover, we have all had human fathers who disciplined us, and we respected them for it. How much more should we submit to the Father of our spirits and live! Our fathers disciplined us for a little while as they thought best; but God disciplines us for our good, that we may share in His holiness.

"No discipline seems pleasant at the time, but painful. Later on, however, it produces a harvest of righteousness and peace for those who have been trained by it. Therefore, strengthen your feeble arms and weak knees. Make level paths for your feet, so that the lame may not be disabled, but rather healed" (NIV).

"The Lord disciplines those He loves" (Hebrews 12:6). I always smile a little when I read this verse. As I rebounded from my failure, at times the discipline felt so severe I would lightheartedly say, "God must love me a lot!" It was grueling at times, and yet the demand He placed on me proved I was a son and belonged to Him. His love for me is unlike any love I have experienced from anyone else. He loves me enough to bring correction, so I end up where I'm supposed to be at the end of my race.

When my children were young and got out of line, I didn't expect someone from the neighborhood to discipline them. They're mine; that's my responsibility. Likewise, I never punished my neighbor's kids because I wasn't their father. They were not my responsibility to the degree that mine were. In the same way, God disciplines His children because He is committed to us. We are His responsibility.

So you can see that God's discipline confirms two things. First, it proves you belong to Him. Discipline is a family affair. When you're disciplined, your Father is dealing with you as His child. This discipline should give you security knowing He's making a way that leads back to where you may have gotten off track. Even better, it points the way forward to a more fulfilling life. If He left you to your own way, there's no telling where you would end up.

Second, discipline confirms His great love for us. Discipline is an expression of His love that matures, rather than His displeasure that penalizes. His goal is to bring us to the place where we can carry the demands of our purpose. God says, "I see greatness in you," and proceeds to hone that greatness through a love that loves enough to discipline.

EVERY ONE EXPERIENCES DISCIPLINE

An unforgettable statement is interjected in the center of Hebrews 12:8. *"And everyone undergoes discipline."* *Everyone* means every person who has a relationship with God will experience some form of discipline. It comes with being family.

The discipline you're experiencing is not God's judgment for your wrong choices. Our bad decisions reap severe consequences, and the choices we made expose areas of weakness in our character. But God disciplines to strengthen, not berate, us. In fact, if we welcome His discipline *before* we make wrong decisions, we'll steer clear of many potential trip-ups.

Discipline is not God subjecting us to His heated anger, but the exposure of His loving arm to come underneath and guide us. When we're beaten up from battle, sometimes a slight nudge is interpreted to be a deliberate punch. Hence, the stuff of life is what God uses to nudge us to keep us from running into a ditch again. Consequently, our overly sensitive, battle-weary selves sometimes take His nudge to be a swing. Isaiah got it right when he wrote the word of the Lord to wearied Israel: *"I will uphold you with My righteous right hand"* (Isaiah 41:10).

Hebrews 12:8 insists that under no circumstances will a son or daughter of God outgrow the need or get a free pass from discipline. The assumption is if you are never corrected you are not *"true sons and daughters at all."* It is part of our growing up, with or without failure. In fact, those who take advantage of His discipline face fewer defeats.

I began playing football when I was thirteen years old and played until I was nearly twenty. In junior high school I learned drills that taught me the fundamentals of the game. When I got to high school, the coach led the team in the same training exercises we learned in junior high. Then I moved on to the next level and began playing college football. I was surprised that on the first day of training our college coach took us through some of the same fundamental drills I learned as a thirteen-year-old junior high player.

Why would a college team use the same drills a junior high team uses? Discipline. Studies show that a team trained in the fundamentals wins more games. Every avenue of life bears this truth, whether it's a career, a hobby, relationships or our spiritual lives. *We become what we repeatedly do.*

The essence of being a disciple of Jesus Christ is submitting to His process of discipline. With each new level of responsibility, God raises the bar in our spiritual life. Therefore, this is not God's "time out" in a corner for His misbehaving kids. It's a common process of life and what God uses to frame our lives and character, for *"Everyone undergoes discipline."*

PREPARED BY THE DISCIPLINE OF A WILDERNESS

The writer of the book of Hebrews addressed Jewish Christians who had become discouraged and nearly given up on following Jesus Christ. They contemplated going back to their old life, giving in to unbelief and returning to Judaism.

The Christian life is not without struggles. The words *"In your struggle against sin"* (v. 4) reveal the rub. The Hebrew believers were not merely struggling with life in general but were severely missing the mark. The writer reminded them that their life in Christ was a marathon that required endurance, but running their race would be impossible if they entertained thoughts of quitting. Hiding their screw-ups and lying to themselves and others by denying their limp only wore them out. Following the Lord brought such persecution to these Hebrews that they threatened to quit following Christ altogether.

I need to note here that not everyone who is rebounding to purpose has fallen to scandalous sin. We get sidetracked by conflicts of a bad marriage, a failed business, job layoffs, disappointment with the church, and on and on it goes. I've experienced struggles with unforgiveness, bitterness, anger and hatred. Whether our action comes from being sinned against, missing the mark ourselves or the mistakes that caused our defeat, we cannot run our race and carry excess baggage. We just aren't built for it. Continually missing the mark stops the flow of life and trips us up from fulfilling our assignment from God. We need strength for our journey, so our heavenly Father uses our struggles to discipline and strengthen us.

After the prophet Samuel anointed young David to be the next king of Israel, David knew God's assignment on his life. And yet David was confined in the caves of Adullam for nearly two decades. If restricted to craggy mountainous caves for years, I would most likely wimp out under the emotional stress. But not David. Instead, he writes, *"By my God I can leap over a wall"* (Psalm 18:29). The discipline David underwent in Adullam became a spiritual and emotional gymnasium. The caves of Adullam prepared David for a crown in Jerusalem.

Discipline looks a lot like a wilderness, even like the one the children of Israel faced after their exodus from Egypt. Once they were free from Egyptian slavery, the children of Israel immediately entered a wilderness. They had lived four hundred years as slaves in Egypt. Their ultimate destiny, however, was to rule and reign in a "land flowing with milk and honey."

Since slaves are not trained to rule, this would require wisdom they did not possess. Many have rightly observed that though the Hebrews no longer lived in Egypt, Egypt was still alive in them.

Getting the Hebrews out of Egypt required the faith and obedience of a man named "Moses." Getting Egypt out of them would require the discipline of a place called "The Wilderness."

Deserts and dying go hand-in-hand, as not a lot of life is found in a desert. Applying this metaphor to us, ways that once worked no longer work. Reliance upon people and things we once trusted in vanish. Our wilderness becomes the sacrificial altar for our Isaacs until the only thing left to depend upon is God Himself.

Discipline is hard, but then it's meant to be. When the children of Israel struck out in search of a promised land, God never warned them the wilderness would become their base of training. Their promised land lay on the other side of the wilderness. Our promise always lies on the other side of discipline. Why does God work this way? His promise is so grand that it would crush us if we tried to carry it before entering the gymnasium of discipline. *You are not just leaving your failure; your failure is leaving you.*

Enduring Hardship as Discipline

The wilderness is a necessary season because God is preparing you for something better. Because religious cultures view God as an overpowering disciplinarian, I feel indebted to reemphasize this point with fresh language. *God is not "whipping you" because of your failure, but "equipping you" to fulfill your assignment.* For this reason, Hebrews 12:7 admonishes battle-weary believers to *"endure hardship."*

We are vulnerable during these seasons. Those of you who have failed may experience rejection from your circle of friends or the distrust of people who once respected you. Confidence may fade as you wander through your desert. The future you thought was secure may appear fleeting. When faced with hardships, it's of utmost importance you realize this important fact. *Your response determines your outcome.*

After I fell, I lost my position as the pastor of a church that, at the time, was the largest and fastest growing church in our city. I could not find employment that was as financially secure, so I struggled to pay the bills. Consequently, my financial credit suffered, and I faced the scrutiny and calls from bill collectors.

One August morning, brilliant rays of sunshine were a welcoming sight when I opened the door leading from our kitchen to the driveway where I parked my car. Everything was routine as I walked out the door to take the children to school. The morning bliss darkened quickly, however, when a tow truck slowly crept into the driveway. My heart began to pound as if it was being pulled out of my chest and stomped on the ground. I knew what the tow truck was there to do. The car payment was overdue, and the bank had sent someone to repossess it. The tow truck wheeled in at seven-thirty in the morning just in time for people to watch the fiasco play out as they passed by on their way to school and work.

With clipboard and pen in hand, the truck driver took long deliberate strides as he made his way from his truck to where I was standing at the driver's side of my car.

Ka-thump. Ka-thump. Ka-thump. The big black boots he wore sounded like logs slamming against the concrete drive.

When he got close enough, he sternly but politely said, "I've come to pick up the car. Would you mind signing this before I put it on the lift?"

"Ye. . .yes." I forced out the words. "Kids, go on back in the house for a minute, and I'll be right in."

With the clipboard in one hand and a blue Bic in the other, he stretched them toward me. I nervously fumbled around trying to clutch the pen between my fingers.

Finding an X that marked the line on the document where I would sign my name, I barely wrote the letters "Willi. . ." when I began shaking. A jolt of hopelessness hit me like a lightning bolt. I wanted to release a torrent of grief and anger on someone, but the only person I knew worthy to receive such a lashing was me.

The burly driver felt my despair. Even I sensed his posture soften as he watched me struggle to sign my name.

I removed my personal belongings, he hooked the car to the tow truck, and I looked on as another part of yesterday's prosperity disappeared over the hill. Another piece of me died that morning as my failure bit another chunk out of my life.

Just then one of the children stuck their head out of the door and asked, "Pop, why is he taking our car?"

Pushing back anger and regret, I swallowed hard. "Our car is broken. He's taking it to the shop to fix it."

Embarrassed in front of my kids, I lied again to cover up another mess. To be honest, I was the one broken. In the days ahead, I would also conclude I was the one who needed fixing.

I was quickly coming to the place everyone calls "rock bottom." The only thing I still had within my power was how I responded to my circumstances. Would I endure this hardship as discipline or react to it as injustice? I settled the issue that I, not other people or God, was responsible for my difficulties. Most were the outcome of what I sowed and now reaped. I chose to receive them as opportunities to make me more dependent on God. By His grace, *I chose to be disciplined by my hardships rather than hardened by the discipline.*

Scripture reveals how God used difficulties to bring discipline to His people. The children of Israel could have left their wilderness in thirteen months. Instead, they remained in it forty years. The apostle Paul explains that they stayed in the desert because they craved evil things, worshipped idols, committed sexual immorality, tempted God and complained about their hardships (1 Corinthians 10:6-10). Thousands died in the wilderness never receiving what God promised them. The attitude we have during our season in the desert of discipline is the factor that determines our outcome.

Choosing to walk through the tough times brings fruitfulness and, in the end, glorifies God. Whether you are reaping hardships from unwise choices you made, or your failure is unattached to any decision you made at all, reap gracefully. God will use the painful seasons to do a more profound work in your life. You have entered a spiritual workout regimen that is preparing you to reign in the midst of your ruins.

THE FOUNDATION OF DISCIPLINE

The foundation of discipline is love. As Hebrews 12:6 says, *"The Lord disciplines those He loves, and He punishes everyone He accepts as a son."* We don't understand discipline as an expression of love because our English word *love* has come to imply indulgence and tolerance. We view discipline and love as opposites. The two central institutions in our nation, our homes and our schools, have renounced the idea of discipline as an act of love.

In the language of the New Testament, the writers could have chosen several words when describing God's love. They decided on *agape* because this word seemed to fit the expression of their experience. Agape views people as God's primary focus and desires the highest good toward those He loves.

Agape is not a mushy love caught up in sheer emotion but loves to the degree it has our ultimate good in mind. God's love has one goal—that we become all He determined us to be. His love prepares us with our future in mind and the fulfillment of our purpose as His focal point.

THE LORD'S HEART FOR THE FALLEN

Even under the Law of Moses, when the Lord addressed fallen Israel His heart to restore them to their purpose overshadowed the Law's demand for justice. Through the prophet Jeremiah, God sends a message to His people who have *once again* failed Him.

> *"For thus says the Lord: 'Your affliction is incurable, your wound is severe. There is no one to plead your cause, that you may be bound up; you have no healing medicines. . . Why do you cry about your affliction? Your sorrow is incurable. Because of the multitude of your iniquities, because your sins have increased, I have done these things to you. . .*
>
> *"'For I will restore health to you and heal you of your wounds,' says the Lord, 'because they called you an outcast saying: "This is Zion; no one seeks her."' Thus says the Lord: 'Behold, I will bring back the captivity of Jacob's tents, and have mercy on his dwelling places; the city shall be built upon its own*

*mound, and the palace shall remain according to its
own plan'"* (Jeremiah 30:12, 15, 17, 18).

Can you sense God's heart through Jeremiah's words? He honestly diagnosed their condition saying, *"Your affliction is incurable;
your wound is severe."* It's a strong statement when God gives the
prognosis as *"incurable."*

Just then He looks again, and through love God's broken heart
cannot leave them in this hopeless condition. Though they are to
blame for their pitiful state, He declares, *"I will restore health to you
and heal your wounds. . .I will bring back the captivity of Jacob's
tents and have mercy on his dwelling places."* Though the Law
condemned their behavior, the Father-heart of God to restore them
overrode its penalty. Even under the Law, *"mercy triumphs over
judgment"* (James 2:13).

God's heart is equally tender toward you. No matter how severe
your wounds may be or how low you have fallen, He is for you.
God does not delight in watching you struggle, even from your
unfaithfulness. He is committed and positioned to rebound your life
and keep you in the game. God's heart throbs with love so deep for
you it heals what may be fatal wounds even you created.

The Hebrew believers are not alone. When our journey becomes
a pathway of discipline, it's common to feel like quitting and return
to our former life. God, however, is on a mission to rebound your
destiny to where you were and even further than before you stumbled and fell. Though it may not seem like it, your divinely arranged
route is leading you into your future. It's working for you, shaping
you, training you and strengthening you. He will not relent until
you walk in His divine intentions. Learn from Israel's wilderness
wanderings and don't give up, complain or turn back. If you do, you
may delay the process or, worse, miss your promised land altogether.

Chapter Nine

Passing the Test of Time

We loathe delays, but in God's world faith requires them. In route to our destiny, the crucible of time refines us until we are ready to carry the responsibility of God's blessing.

L ife is the brief experience we have while living in a multi-dimensional reality we call "time." Our time on earth is fleeting, for we will not live in these human bodies forever. The psalmist wrote, *"I wither away like grass"* (Psalm 102:11). Even so, God chose our withering frame as the dwelling place of His eternal, timeless Spirit. No wonder that throughout the ages every culture on the planet has revered and, at times, idolized this thing called "time."

History can be an excellent teacher, but it's not a roommate we should cozy up with forever. It's just not wise to live with something (or someone) that no longer exists. Our dreams, on the other hand, wait for us in the future. If we idly waste the present, however, while contemplating past triumphs or regrets, and think future dreams will just happen, we're fooling ourselves. How we steward *time* is essential.

In the words of the preacher of Ecclesiastes, *"To everything there is a season, a time for every purpose under heaven"* (Ecclesiastes 3:1). It's not merely a "wise old saying." This is a promise from God. The preacher gives hope that *"every purpose"* (this includes yours) has an assigned time of fulfillment. Think of the possibilities! *"Every purpose under heaven"* will have its season when the Almighty says, "Now. . .," and suddenly, divine favor manifests dreams and destinies. Only God knows His *"now,"* and yet there is a connection between how we steward our time and when He fulfills His.

MATURING IS A PROCESS OF TIME

Growing up, "Uncle Claude" was my favorite uncle. I suppose every family has a crazy uncle, and Uncle Claude was ours. He always seemed to show up at our house when Mom was serving supper. Uncle Claude could say the most stupid things at the wrong time and cause a family ruckus. Then he would do something for you or make you laugh, and you would love him again. I always felt as if I was Uncle Claude's favorite too.

When I was twelve years old, my favorite crazy uncle decided the time had come for me to learn to drive a car. Not in the driveway, but on the road! Of course, I was all over this idea.

Uncle Claude's snub-nosed Ford Econoline truck was perfect for a twelve-year-old to see the road well enough to steer the truck. After giving me a thirty-minute lesson on how to shift gears (a straight-drive on the column—three-on-the-tree), he assured me I was ready to solo.

Here we went, easing onto Spring Garden Avenue, the little road that stretched in front of his house. Uncle Claude sat in the passenger's seat cackling when I choked the truck down three times while trying to get the hang of synchronizing the clutch and gears. My crazy uncle was in tears laughing as the little truck "hopped" down the road on my maiden voyage.

Now pause a moment and think this through. Uncle Claude was getting a kick out of teaching his twelve-year-old nephew to drive a truck on the road. What's even crazier, I got the hang of it and learned to drive. After a while, I would beg him to let me behind the wheel, and it was nothing for me to make the half-mile trip down Spring Garden Avenue from his house to the community store.

Here's the lesson. While I *knew how* to drive Uncle Claude's truck at twelve, I was not mature enough to handle the responsibility of *being* a driver. *Knowing* and *being* are different. Waiting for the day when I would turn sixteen and get my driver's license seemed like an eternity. The process of aging from twelve to sixteen would test me severely. Likewise, God knows the time when we're ready to bear the burden of His promised purpose. Even when we understand because we know what to do, God knows when we are mature enough to carry the responsibility.

Paul reminds us that Abraham *"through faith and patience inherited the promises"* (Hebrews 6:12). God promised him he would have an heir, and yet he and Sarah were childless into their old age. They knew, but the time had not arrived for the promise to materialize. *Faith* and *patience* were the weapons Abraham used as he squared off against time. Spiritual arsenals are necessary when time puts us to the test.

REBOUNDING FROM A FALL REQUIRES TIME

I'm convinced Adam's fall transpired over time. The serpent captured Eve's attention in the garden, and I imagine Eve having a conversation with the devil for days or months, perhaps years. However time was measured in those days, the fall was a process rather than an isolated event.

Eve's private conversation with the devil was how he stuck his foot in the doorway of her mind. Each time she gave the serpent an audience, his suggestions and questions weakened her a little more. Reading the story can give the impression the devil blindsided Eve. Don't believe it. Adam and Eve's failure developed over time before they acted upon the suggestions of the evil one.

The process of failure hasn't changed. It plays out the same way through our lives today. It rarely occurs in a moment but is a collection of thoughts and suggestions we entertain over time. An idea here, a temptation there, we compromise, and then—Wham! The effects appear suddenly, but they transpired over time.

THE TEST OF TIME

If history teaches anything, we come to realize the immensity of our loss and, in particular, how much time we have lost. It's only natural not to want to waste any more time and get back to normal as quickly as possible. So we face two extremes. First, we contemplate giving up and not coming back at all. As I expressed at length in chapter 8, the journey appears too overwhelming and wearisome. Second, we are tempted to take matters into our own hands and rush the process. Indeed, there is *"a time for every purpose under heaven,"* but the mystery of *when* is what we have to leave with God, and therein lies the test.

As discussed in chapter 2, the moment Adam and Eve fell God set in motion a plan to pursue them. The Father immediately set humanity on a path that would restore everything. After their fall, all of God's creation became aware of the ticking clock as it awaits the day when everything will rebound to God's original purpose.

As the story of humanity unfolds, you may wonder why God didn't act sooner. Why the wait? He promised to send the seed of the woman (Genesis 3:15), so where was this Seed of promise?

I am not sure anyone but God knows the answer to this mystery. But Scripture says, *"When the fullness of the time had come, God sent forth His Son, born of a woman, under the law, to redeem those who were under the law, that we might receive the adoption as sons"* (Galatians 4:4). When everything was right, Jesus Christ showed up to restore everything and everyone to the destiny God intended from the beginning of time.

When Moses led Israel through the wilderness, their most significant test was not the Red Sea or the lack of food and water, but time. The people pressed Moses to make life normal again. For more than four hundred years, however, their "normal" had been slavery. Many Israelites chose their familiar routine of slavery over taking time to walk through the wilderness to prepare them for their God-given promise. The children of Israel became so engrossed with what was *not* happening that they missed what God was doing as they walked through the wilderness. As time passed, so did faith and patience, and many of them let the promise slip away.

*"Now when the people saw that Moses **delayed coming down from the mountain,** the people gathered together to Aaron, and said to him, 'Come, make us gods that shall go before us; for as for this Moses, the man who brought us up out of the land of Egypt, we do not know what has become of him.'"*
(Exodus 32:1, bold added)

The Israelites took things into their own hands so they could "get on with life." While Moses stayed hidden away on the mountain for forty days and nights, the children of Israel failed the test. They convinced Aaron to make a golden calf, and afterward they celebrated with a party that led them into idolatry and all manner of wickedness. The saying "Just get on with your life" has positive and negative consequences. The positive is that we don't become idle. The negative, we take time into our own hands when we should humbly leave it to God. When Israel grew weary trudging through the wilderness the test of time exposed their calloused hearts. We will all face the same examination.

As I read the story of Moses and Israel, I'm amazed at how they could look at a golden statue molded from the jewelry they once wore and proclaim, *"'This is your god, O Israel, that brought you out of the land of Egypt!' So when Aaron saw it, he built an altar before it. And Aaron made a proclamation and said, 'Tomorrow is a feast to the Lord'"* (Exodus 32:4-5). Even after seeing the tangible, manifest glory of God hover above them day and night, Aaron declared that a calf made from their own gold jewelry was the *"god. . .that brought you out of the land of Egypt!"*

The lesson? Impatience warps reality. When faith wanes because of delay, we will be tempted either to quit (return to Egypt) or to build a golden calf and worship it. If we abandon the process, we opt for dying in the wilderness. But if our twisted reality leads us to build an idol, it can look a lot like God. Either way we forfeit God's promise.

Loyal friends may boost our confidence and encourage us to accept God's forgiveness and move on. These are usually people who genuinely love us in spite of our failures. While I commend

95

their love and loyalty, hear a word of caution. Often, this is a golden calf that's contrived during our delays. Well-meaning people who love us will pass the hat to collect enough gold to build something that, at the moment, can look a lot like God. Noble causes and ministries are often golden calves that someone created after they've failed the test of time. Someone suggests we leave our appointment with counseling, the hospital, the treatment center, and on it goes. It's not that the choices are sinfully wrong; they may just be out of step with God's time.

Healing the Soul Takes Time

Forgiveness comes the moment we ask God to forgive us, but I've discovered it takes time to heal a wounded soul. Forgiveness has to do with believing. Repairing the heart, on the other hand, involves walking out the grace we experienced through His mercy. Do not confuse being forgiven with being restored. Jesus provides forgiveness at the cross. Rebounding from failure is a process. Forgiveness comes in an instant, but our hearts recover over time.

As a boy, my dad restored wrecked cars. Dad was a gifted mechanic and auto body repairman and earned money on the side repairing broken-down vehicles. It wasn't strange to see him come from work pulling an old car with the hood and grill smashed in from a past collision. I looked at his dilapidated trophies he pulled home and asked Mom, "What possesses him to buy these piles of junk?"

In no time, Dad would go to work on the old rag-of-a-car. He would beat, hammer and sand on it for months until it took shape. When it was ready, he sprayed on a few coats of paint, and the finished product looked exactly like the manufacturer's original design. It was remarkable to witness Dad restore these broken-down vehicles. From the junkyards to the highways, he was a master at repairing wrecks. The process, however, was time-consuming.

When Jesus purchased us, we too looked pretty gruesome when He pulled us home the first time. Through Jesus, God redeems us and makes us His own. We belong to Him. Jesus Christ *"purchased men unto God from every tribe and language and people and nation"*

(Revelation 5:9, Amplified Bible). After all, He designed us, and He knows how to restore us to His original design. Paul says we are *"bought at a price"* (1 Corinthians 6:20), and that price was the blood of Jesus Christ He shed on the cross.

The moment my dad purchased a wrecked vehicle, he was not concerned about its condition. Now it was his. He rarely found out how the cars became smashed up in the first place, when it happened or who was at fault. In fact, he didn't care. Their decrepit shape was what attracted him to them in the first place.

The wreck now belonged to Dad, so it wasn't enough for him merely to have his name on the title. His goal was to get it back on the road to do what it was created to do. He planned a rebound for the old jalopy. Restoring it to its original purpose, however, would require time for him to work his miracle and make it happen.

You belong to the Father. He purchased your life through the death of His Son, Jesus. He brought you to Himself forgiven and yet broken. Because you are His, He will never leave you or forsake you in your brokenness. Never. He is committed to working with you until you are restored to fulfill your purpose and walk in the destiny He prepared for you all along.

OUR CHRONOS VS. GOD'S KAIROS

Most people are not aware that we live within two spheres of time. One is called *Chronos*, the other *Kairos*. *Chronos* and *Kairos* are Greek words used in the New Testament; both are translated as "time" in our English language. *Chronos* signifies measurable time like the date on a calendar or the hours on a clock. *Chronos* is the root of our English word *chronology*.

Kairos, on the other hand, portrays a "God time" that can't be measured but only shows up at an appropriate and chosen moment in history. Galatians 4:4 says, *"But when the fullness of time had come, God sent forth His Son. . . ."* The *"fullness of time"* is God's *Kairos*. We celebrate our Lord's birth in Bethlehem on December 25 (though this was not the actual date of His birth). The year we celebrate is *Chronos*, but the fact that God chose a time for His Son to

97

be born of a virgin in Bethlehem is *Kairos*. The *Chronos* (December 25) is not nearly as crucial as *Kairos*, God's chosen moment. When the time had come on God's calendar, heaven's time intersected with our time, and this resulted in the miracle we call Christmas.

One of my spiritual fathers, the late Dr. Charles Cookman, preached a sermon many who knew him considered to be his life message. He titled it *What's Happening Is Not What's Going On!* The title of the sermon *was* the message.

The sermon reflected on the life of Joseph recorded in Genesis 37. Joseph had a dream of destiny for his life. Being the favored son of his father, Jacob, his brothers steamed with such jealousy they threw Joseph into a pit in the wilderness and sold him to a group of Ishmaelite traders. In turn, they sold him as a servant-slave to an officer in Egypt named Potiphar. Joseph's faithfulness to Potiphar would set him up to be a trusted servant only to be framed and lied about by Potiphar's wife when he refused her sexual advances. Joseph was then put in prison to pull time for a crime he didn't commit.

While in prison, he faithfully served his fellow inmates by giving accurate interpretations of their dreams about their future. Joseph's only request to one inmate was that he would remember him and put in a good word for him to Pharaoh when he was released. But his fellow prisoner forgot all about Joseph. Once again, Joseph was being tested and prepared by time.

As the years passed, Joseph never forgot the God-inspired dream he had when he was seventeen years old, for therein lay his purpose and destiny. Throughout Joseph's hard circumstances, the story unfolds to reveal that what was happening was not what was going on. Joseph's unbearable hard time was demanding and profoundly unjust. In the unseen realm of the Spirit, however, what was going on was the making of a man who would have the character to bear the weight of his future purpose. Joseph's hard time prepared him to carry a divine favor that would set him up to lead nations.

As life played out for Joseph, God's favor on his life promoted him from being a prisoner to being prime minister of Egypt. Looking back on his hardships, Joseph wisely declared, *"God meant it for good, in order to bring it about as it is this day, to save many people alive"* (Genesis 50:20). When Joseph's *Chronos* crossed paths with God's *Kairos,* his dream became his reality.

The same thing is transpiring with you. You may see hurt, pain, brokenness, shame and loss (to name a few). You may wonder when your pain will subside or the depression lift or your reputation be restored. What's going on can't be witnessed or judged by what you see or feel. The Holy Spirit is working with you and for you. God has not forgotten you. Time is passing, but He is in the midst of it positioning everything for a *Kairos* moment. Jesus already rebounded your missed shot when He died on the cross and resurrected from the grave. The *Chronos* has taken place, and now, though the hammering and sanding are uncomfortable, you're being restored to the image God created in the first place. You are rebounding into your place of destiny.

SURRENDERING YOUR WAY TO VICTORY

David faced this process in the years that followed his failures. He created not one but several personal disasters that caused him pain and nearly his position as the king of Israel. After committing adultery with Bathsheba, his conspiracy to kill her husband and faithful general, Uriah, are the failures where David gets the most press. As if this is not enough to overcome, later he faces the agony of his children in rebellion and in particular his son, Absalom. In Psalm 31:10-13, the great king of Israel anguishes over his circumstances.

> *"For my life is spent with grief, and my years with sighing; my strength fails because of my iniquity, and my bones waste away. I am a reproach among all my enemies, but especially among my neighbors, and am repulsive to my acquaintances; those who see me outside flee from me. I am forgotten like a dead man, out of mind; I am like a broken vessel. For I hear the slander of many; fear is on every side; while they take counsel together against me, they scheme to take away my life."*

Most scholars agree that David penned these words after he committed adultery with Bathsheba and conspired the death of her husband, Uriah. As he writes, he's now facing his kingdom being divided and taken by Absalom's rebellion. These are the gut-wrenching words of a man trying to push through the depressing consequences of the disaster he created.

Even so, David found the secret passageway out of his maze of confusion. His discovery is our antidote to the rollercoaster that entices us to try harder, repent more sincerely or try to prove ourselves to those who watched us lose our way.

Like Joseph before him, David raised the white flag of surrender to God. He yielded his way to victory with God and man.

> *"But as for me, I trust in You, O Lord; I say, 'You are my God.'* **My times are in Your hand;** *deliver me from the hand of my enemies, and from those who persecute me. Make Your face shine upon Your servant; save me for Your mercies' sake"* (Psalm 31:14-16, bold added).

David had learned the value of surrendering to God's timing. The prophet Samuel anointed David in his teenage years to be Israel's king. He had several opportunities to push himself into that position and on numerous occasions was encouraged by his fellow warriors to do so. Several times he could have justifiably killed Saul. Even then, David released his destiny into the hands of God. He wisely waited for God's timing as he worked through the hardship and unjust treatment he experienced.

Now, under different circumstances, David recalled the lessons. He laid down manipulation and surrendered the outcome to God. Knowing it was the presence of God that gave him victory over the lion, the bear and Goliath, losing the Presence was what David feared most. He knew that if he surrendered his time to God His face would shine upon him again.

We find freedom in releasing our times to God. Surrendering our times to Him, past and future, frees us to experience life to the full today. Freedom comes when we release into God's hands the remorse of what could have been and the uncertainties of what might be. Once you do, you cease striving to prove your value and rest in the fact that God values you now, and that's enough.

What's happening?

God has positioned you in the uncomfortable place of a vanishing past and an unrealized future. Time you can never recoup has slipped away, and the promise is yet to come.

What's *really* going on?

God is prying your hands away from controlling your own destiny. He is taking bits of your life and forming you like a Joseph, a David or possibly an Esther. In the stillness of time, when you think nothing is happening, if you will be still you will hear your Father say, "Trust Me, and watch what I do with the rest of your life."

Chapter Ten

Sweetening the Bitter Waters

Bitterness is a root that burrows deep beneath the surface of the heart. It feeds on thoughts and feelings from a painful past and stealthily grows into a monstrous beast. If this is only the root, imagine what it will become if it's not pulled up and thrown out.

About a year and a half had passed since my life imploded due to a moral failure. I had to leave a vital church that, on two separate occasions, I had led for a total of ten years.

After a Sunday worship service in a church my wife and I were attending in a neighboring city, we lingered and chatted with people. Just then I spotted a lady and her husband, members of the church I had left, walking toward us. Seeing their eager smiles sparked a barrage of feelings. Embarrassment and disgust surfaced within me as my emotions churned. Picture the mouth of a volcano with red-hot lava swirling and spitting up fumes from hell just before it erupts. That's about as close as I can come to describing my reaction as they swaggered in our direction.

The lady was one of those endlessly cheery types, an over-the-top sanguine personality. Her husband was quite the opposite, unassuming and melancholy in nature.

"Hey, guys! How are you?! We want you to know we love you guys!" (The exclamations are intentional but still don't come close to her irritating voice inflections.)

My response surprised my wife. For the most part, I'd always been able to rein in my thoughts before responding. But this time the "stuff" brewing inside me leaped the walls of my gregarious nature. In a split second I puked my boiling emotions all over her. I know, sounds terrible. The timing of volcanic eruptions is like that—unexpected and scary. Anyone in the way becomes charred from the heat and toxins of such outbursts.

I had come to despise being pitied, primarily by former church members who expressed sympathy for my recent condition. If I met an old church member and they said, "I love you," I interpreted that to mean, "Because of what you did, *I feel sorry for you.*" The malice inside me tainted my view of people, and even life itself. Warm expressions of friendliness from specific people easily offended me. The real problem, however, boiled within my own soul. I felt that I had disappointed God, my family, my closest friends, people who trusted me, the city where I pastored and even myself. And, frankly, I didn't know what to do about it.

As we drove home, my wife broke the silence and asked, "Where did *that* come from?" I was completely unaware of a problem. Honestly, I was somewhat proud of myself for reacting so strongly to someone I considered to be another smiling, religious do-gooder.

She continued. "They just wanted to be nice and speak to us. Surely you know they probably felt just as awkward approaching us as we felt seeing them. After all, they were sitting in the back row. We didn't even know they were at the church service, so they could have slipped out without saying anything. They chose to speak to us."

Like cancer, bitterness can lie dormant before it surfaces. This emotional infection can stay deceitfully hidden, slowly contaminating the human spirit. In fact, to prove just how deceitful it can be, the poisonous gall flared up in me right after I had worshipped God. Bitterness mingled with worship, went undetected in the same heart. It took a while, but I finally owned the fact that my explosive response came from bitterness that had been growing inside me for almost two years.

EFFECTS OF HIDDEN HOSTILITY

Bitterness contaminates the soul and, eventually, the whole personality. It's unrealistic to expect to go through life without opportunities to become bitter over life's experiences. In truth, the more numerous our relationships, the more vulnerable we are to being hurt. An offense is almost always the means used to strike and infect us. Jesus' words *"offenses must come"* (Matthew 18:7) prove it's impossible to follow Him without having these confrontations. Christ did not say they "may come" but *"must come."*

The question we need to ask is, what will we do when they come? The answer is cliché, but true nonetheless. We allow them to make us better or bitter. God can use an offense to begin the process of eradicating our selfish egotistic nature. It's what the apostle Paul meant when he wrote, *"I am crucified with Christ"* (Galatians 2:20). When we are willing to die *"with Christ"* or, to say it another way, " like Christ," only then can we say with Paul, *"Nevertheless I live"* (Galatians 2:20).

Dying to our need to be right and surrendering those rights rooted in our ego are the pathway of Christ. On the surface, it may appear we have suffered significant losses by relinquishing our rights to defend ourselves. But in reality this is when we are most in control of our destiny. We've surrendered our attempts to strive against people and circumstances and plotted our course with the confidence of peace. Paul's willingness to abandon his rights and be crucified with Christ is how the old apostle could confidently proclaim, *"I live."*

When you think about it, dead men are the most liberated of all people. When you kill the opportunity to become bitter over life's hard circumstances, you exude more life than ever. As bitterness is released, nothing remains for evil to work with, and the Lord can deal with the real issue at hand. . .*you.*

Bitterness affects three persons (or personalities): the Holy Spirit, your relationships and yourself. To the believers in Ephesus, Paul wrote,

"And do not grieve the Holy Spirit of God, by whom you were sealed for the day of redemption. Let all bitterness, wrath, anger, clamor, and evil speaking be put away from you, with all malice. And be kind to one another, tenderhearted, forgiving one another, just as God in Christ forgave you" (Ephesians 4:30-32).

The Holy Spirit grieves in the presence of bitterness. The word *grieve* could also be rendered "to cause to be heavy, sad or sorrowful." Harboring resentment hinders our relationship with the Holy Spirit. It's not that He leaves us, for we can never escape Him. But we lose joy because we feel His sadness. There's an intermingledness, a oneness between the Holy Spirit and our spirit. So the feelings of one affect the other. Maybe this explains why a depressive atmosphere covers us. We are sensing the Holy Spirit's grief.

Harbored bitterness affects everyone who comes in contact with us. For this reason, Paul said, *"And be kind to one another, tender-hearted, forgiving one another, just as God in Christ forgave you."* The people you do life with are part of you. We are *"members of one another"* (Romans 12:5). If the smallest member of the body has an infection, the whole body will feel it and can even become infected. Paul instructed the church in Ephesus to be kind and forgiving to one another because these are the virtues that counteract bitterness, wrath, anger, clamor, evil speaking and malice. Kindness and forgiveness are antidotes against these malicious poisons.

BITTERNESS DEFINED

Bitterness is a spiritual and emotional cancer. As cancer cells are to the physical body, bitterness is to the soul. Like renegade cancer cells, it secretly cohabits with healthy parts of the body. When healthy cells live with the infected ones, the healthy cells are in danger of being contaminated and join the rebellion. Like cancer, bitterness can be undetected for years. Its strategy is to distort and destroy the beautiful and original design God intended for our lives.

Bitterness carries a voracious appetite for revenge. When our pain feels unbearable, our suppressed hostility yearns for the people we think are responsible for it to feel the same despair we are experiencing. Unfulfilled bitterness goes unsatisfied until it dines at the banqueting table of revenge. Undisturbed, resentment marinates in memories, and after a season of meditating on our trouble, the gall gushes forth.

Hebrews 12:14-16 gives insight into bitterness and how it lives within us.

> *"Pursue peace with all people, and holiness, without which no one will see the Lord: looking diligently lest anyone fall short of the grace of God; lest any root of bitterness springing up cause trouble, and by this many become defiled; lest there be any fornicator or profane person like Esau, who for one morsel of food sold his birthright."*

This passage calls bitterness a *root* that sinks its tentacles into the cavernous soil of our heart while we stew over the injustice we suffered. The more we meditate on our despair, the deeper it goes. Over time, the root becomes a channel that nourishes the offense. Consequently, those who befriend us because of our pain and take our offense upon themselves are also prone to be infected.

Like the root of a mighty oak, bitter roots demand nourishment. The roots travel along and feed upon the sympathy of people. If we do not stop feeding it, as the writer of Hebrews says, the root will *"spring up"* and display its fruit of distorted attitudes and behaviors. Even medical professionals agree that bitterness can manifest itself through various physical ailments.

THE BITTER ROOT OF FAILURE

Unresolved bitterness never finds closure. A bitter root can come, not only from offenses received, but those committed. It's not unusual to hold self-hatred for allowing a situation that caused us to fall and our life to spin out of control.

We find a classic example in the story of the twin brothers, Jacob and Esau (Genesis 25-27). Esau, the firstborn, by tradition was to receive the birthright and blessing of his father, Isaac. By ancient customs the inheritance of a father's blessing was a big deal. Jacob, the younger twin, was obsessed with obtaining the blessing that rightfully belonged to his brother. Their story reveals he would go to any length to get it. Eventually, he went so far as to deceive his older brother and father, thus living up to the name, Jacob—deceiver and usurper.

After Esau had spent the day hunting, Jacob took advantage of the opportunity to lure his tired, hungry brother into trading his birthright for a mere meal of lentil stew. With his belly and appetite satisfied, Scripture states, *"Esau despised his birthright"* (Genesis 25:34). His temporary food craving blinded him to his future destiny with his father's blessing. The cry of present hunger silenced the voice of future promise. Fleeting pleasures have a way of usurping our future by demanding temporary relief.

As Isaac approached his death, he called for Esau to bring him a freshly cooked meal. Afterward he would give his elder son his blessing and then die.

Jacob, ruthlessly wanting the family blessing, with the help of his mother, deceived a nearly blind, elderly Isaac into believing he was Esau. Jacob's mother prepared the meal Jacob served to his father and then readied himself to receive the blessing. Thinking he was blessing his firstborn son, Esau, the weak-eyed old man passed the family lineage to the younger, more ambitious Jacob.

After Jacob received his father's blessing and birthright, the Genesis account captures the heartwrenching exchange between Esau and his father, Jacob.

> *"When Esau heard the words of his father, he cried with an exceedingly great and bitter cry, and said to his father, 'Bless me—me also, O my father!'*
>
> *"But he said, 'Your brother came with deceit and has taken away your blessing.'*

*"And Esau said, 'Is he not rightly named Jacob?
For he has supplanted me these two times. He took
away my birthright, and now look, he has taken away
my blessing!' And he said, 'Have you not reserved a
blessing for me?'*

*"Then Isaac answered and said to Esau, 'Indeed
I have made him your master, and all his brethren
I have given to him as servants; with grain and
wine I have sustained him. What shall I do now for
you, my son?'*

*"So Esau hated Jacob because of the blessing
with which his father blessed him, and Esau said
in his heart, 'The days of mourning for my father
are at hand; then I will kill my brother Jacob'"*
(Genesis 27:34-37, 41).

As wrong as Jacob's deceit appears to be, our issue is with Esau's indifference. Jacob was far more passionate for his father's blessing and the birthright than Esau. Esau's apathy toward fulfilling the legacy as the elder brother caused him to surrender his destiny at the altar of passing hunger. It reasons that the worst deceit Esau suffered did not come from his twin brother, Jacob, but from himself.

The moment Esau realized what he had lost, *"He cried with an exceedingly great and bitter cry."* The words *"So Esau hated Jacob"* reveal how bitterness became lodged in Esau's heart.

When we fall and sacrifice our God-given purpose, we may be tempted to turn outward on others and excessively inward on ourselves. In Esau's case, he allowed the bitter root of hatred to grow toward Jacob and blamed all his trouble on his brother's deceit. He didn't look at himself and realize that if he had esteemed his purpose and refused to surrender to the appetite of his flesh his future would still be awaiting him.

It can be staggering when we become aware of what we lost from our fall. We can become bitter at the "Jacobs" who fill roles and positions we once occupied or were in line to fill. I do believe we have a spiritual enemy that wants us angry at God, blaming Him for allowing the tragedy to transpire in the first place. Our enemy's strategy is to get us to focus on everyone involved and blame our present condition on someone else. These can, indeed, be days of intense spiritual warfare.

WE BECOME WHAT WE BEHOLD

The Old Testament book of Ruth tells the story of Naomi, who, after losing her husband and two sons to untimely deaths, was left alone with no way to make a living. Being a destitute widow, she reacted to her harsh circumstances in bitterness. To her credit, it shows that she at least recognized her condition when she said to Ruth, *"Don't call me Naomi; call me Mara, for the Almighty has dealt very bitterly with me"* (Ruth 1:20).

Her name, *Naomi,* means "pleasant." After her difficulties, however, she was not at all pleasant. Naomi became so bitter she demanded that people call her "Mara," which means "bitter." Naomi illustrates how it is possible to become bitter to the degree we focus upon the circumstances that have hurt us.

You can see the principle behind this in 2 Corinthians 3:18.

"But we all. . .beholding as in a mirror the glory of the Lord, are being transformed into the same image from glory to glory, just as by the Spirit of the Lord."

In a nutshell, "we become what we behold." No one is born bitter. When a person focuses on their tragic circumstances, in due time they are a reflection of the pain of their fixation.

Naomi focused on the loss of loved ones and her means of living, and the outlook became evident on her countenance. What happened to her can happen to any of us if we muse over our mess. No wonder when someone surrenders to a bitter spirit, we say, "They are bitter." Like Naomi, in many respects "Bitter" becomes their name.

THE SOLUTION

I religiously rehearsed my failure and the rejections of people who once respected me. Like Esau, I hated myself for stroking the present passions of my flesh, rather than submitting to the future purposes of God. But I also hated the characters in my story, the Jacobs I once loved and enjoyed. I wish they had only worn their disappointment on their sleeve, but most wore it on their faces. When I met them in public, their scowled stares fed the fires of bitterness inside me even more. A more profound disdain grew toward them for rejecting me, but it also deepened because I felt the guilt of giving them a reason to believe as they did.

Take my advice and *stop looking back to rehearse your pain.* Replaying your failure, the losses and people's rejection does nothing but brew a pot of lentil stew that feeds the disappointment in you and your contempt for them.

Praying for and speaking a blessing to others is a powerful solution to bitterness. Instead of rehearsing those negative and painful memories, come at it from another angle. Through praise and thanksgiving to God, start praying for others who hold your mistakes against you. Choose to release words of blessing over their life. In fact, Jesus instructed us to do this.

> *"But I say to you, love your enemies, **bless those who curse you**, do good to those who hate you, and pray for those who spitefully use you and persecute you, that you may be sons of your Father in heaven"* (Matthew 5:44-45, bold added).

At first, you may think you're hypocritical, even insincere, praying something you do not sincerely feel or wish would happen. If we are honest, most of us don't want God to bless the people who will not forgive us. Since bitterness demands revenge, we want them to hurt to the same degree we do. You will be stunned, however, as you intentionally and "out loud" bless the people who are against you; love for them will begin to grow. It's impossible to hate the people you consistently pray for God to bless.

One of the most challenging situations I had to overcome after I fell came when my best friend publicly spoke against me. Previously, he openly stated he would stand by my side even if I were guilty of the alleged accusations. As it turned out, I *was* guilty, but he was not loyal to his word and quite the opposite. When I went from being one of the most popular people in my city to being the most talked about, he changed his tune. Instead of standing with me in my pain, he publicly spoke evil of me, making my lousy situation even worse.

To top it off, I had to drive by his home every day. When I did, my mind would press the replay button and rehearse the good times we had together. These scenes faded, and unpleasant ones came up. These recalled him speaking against me. The devil knows how to use the grapevine so every discouraging remark people have uttered against us finds its way to our ears. Hearing what my friend said about me to others crushed my spirit, sending me into a tailspin of depression.

After reading Matthew 5:44-45, I sensed the Holy Spirit leading me to bless him and his family verbally every time I passed their home. I do not have the language to express how difficult this was for me to do. Even so, I knew it was right. So, with all the sincerity I could muster, which, by the way, wasn't much, I did it. Calling out the name of my friend, his wife and children, I prayed for them, asking God to bless them, and then *I blessed them*. In the beginning, it felt formal and insincere, but I sensed the pleasure of God upon it. I imagined angels looking at one another, smiling, and saying, "He's on his way back now." Over time the hardness of my heart softened, and the more I prayed this way, the easier it became.

After a while, blessing those who cursed me became as natural as praying a blessing over dinner, and I found myself looking forward to praying for them. As I prayed for my friends to be blessed, I was getting blessed. The clouds of bitterness that covered me broke up. Blessing my friend, who had become an enemy, poked a hole through the dark atmosphere that hung over me and severed the umbilical cord that fed the bitter root.

The prayer of blessing upon those who curse you is a key that unlocks the door to free you. I want to emphasize that this is not some magic formula or a "hocus pocus" incantation. Praying a blessing is to become our lifestyle and the way we pray for others. It especially applies during the challenging seasons when we are living in the hard times of our own failures.

SWEETEN THE BITTER WATER

In the wilderness the children of Israel became thirsty. The only water they could find was bitter water at a place called "Marah." Look familiar? It should. It's the same name Naomi gave herself after the death of her husband and sons left her an impoverished widow.

If the children of Israel drank the waters of Marah, it would kill them. I think I've sufficiently made the point that drinking from bitter waters always brings a slow death.

So Moses *"cried out to the Lord and the Lord showed him a tree"* (Exodus 15:25a). I'm not sure how Moses was prompted to do what he did next. Even so, *"when he cast it into the waters, the waters were made sweet"* (Exodus 15:25b). This tree was a revelation of the cross of Jesus revealed centuries before its time.

There is a tree that purifies the putrid water of life's sorrows. This tree is the eternal cross where Jesus died for our failures, including *our bitterness*. The horrible shortcomings that speak of our defeat become the place of our most magnificent victory. When we choose to apply Christ's cross to the bitter waters of our life and view our failures through His death and resurrection, grace comes to forgive and deliver.

Your most bitter places of defeat and failure can become the sweetest places of triumph. People will take notice of how your fallen, soured life has become sweeter than they could ever imagine. You will be a testimony of how someone with a failure like yours can become a well of sweetened waters where people come to drink and live. Oddly enough, the scars from your fall will be the very reason so many will trust your message of hope and resurrection.

Chapter Eleven

Despising the Shame

Shame controls us by pointing to our failures, making us feel unacceptable, less valuable and lovable. This enemy holds us captive when we remain silent and isolated, but it cowers before the courageous soul who dares to get up and try again, weaknesses and all.

The smooth autumn breeze whistled between the trees loosening leaves from their branches. It looked as if it were raining gold as the morning sunshine bounced off the foliage that playfully danced its way to the ground. It was so beautiful I planned to enjoy the crisp fall day as it came to me. Driving to a local grocery store to pick up a few things, I found myself piddling through the store aisles looking at nothing in particular. Suddenly, fear ricocheted through my heart when I looked up to see a familiar face glaring at me. Our eyes met for a split second; then she quickly looked away as though she didn't see me. That millisecond encounter shifted my golden morning to one of dark hopelessness. It felt like one of those dreams when you find yourself stark naked in a public place with nowhere to hide. Like Jonah's whale, shame swallowed me up and buried me so deeply in a belly of darkness that I darted for the next aisle and out the door.

The sky was still bright and blue just as it was when I entered the store ten minutes earlier. But suddenly, out of nowhere, the disapproving presence of one woman, a former church member, caused an eclipse of darkness to fall on me. One look at the "shame on you" scowl on her face and my day was over.

HOUSE ARREST

Shame is the go-to weapon most often used when people have disappointed us or disgraced our value system. Religion uses shame as a judicial system uses house arrest. House arrest limits alleged felons by locking an ankle bracelet on them that allows authorities to track them should they venture beyond their assigned location. All is well as long as they stay within their designated boundaries. But if they do not, the device electronically signals headquarters and the authorities go looking for them.

In place of an ankle bracelet, shame attached itself to my heart and emotions. I had fallen from the very values I preached and esteemed important. I'm sure it wasn't entirely accurate, but it felt like former church members were assigned to keep me in my place.[3] Though I tried to apologize to people I thought I should go to, apologies were not enough. They seemed to fall short especially when those who once looked up to me heard of my admitted guilt. When I bumped into them in public, the rejection they expressed worked like a tracking system that set off a siren of shame. Shame sent out a blaring signal that I had been spotted taking advantage of my freedom. Soon the "shame police" would find me, give me "the look," and I would dart back into seclusion. I know this wasn't actually how it happened; but to me, this was how it felt.

I had sincerely confessed my failure as thoroughly as I knew how to at the time, and yet I remained incarcerated. Religious shame believes we can be forgiven when we fall and still go to heaven when we die. But it also teaches that severe cases carry a "life sentence" for the remainder of our time on earth. For these, we must forfeit our God-given purpose and destiny. It's a type of house arrest that scolds you if you don't stay in your place or, worse, penalizes you if you attempt to do life as you did before you made a mess of things. How can God receive us into His holy heaven and yet penalize us for our remaining days on an ungodly planet? I've always been puzzled by such logic.

Of all the emotions I experienced after my fall, shame was the most degrading. It was a new and powerful enemy I had never faced before. Though I didn't grow up in a church-going family, I could never remember feeling so unaccepted and unworthy of being loved. No amount of confession was enough to outrun the foreboding shadow of shame that made me feel like a disgraceful piece of crap.

JESUS DESPISED SHAME

I had read this passage of Scripture hundreds of times. And yet one day I saw it for the first time. Three words permitted me to declare war against this foe and forever changed my perspective of God's regard to shame.

> *"Looking unto Jesus, the author and finisher of our faith, who for the joy that was set before Him endured the cross, **despising the shame**, and has sat down at the right hand of the throne of God"* (Hebrews 12:2, bold added).

The writer nestled these words in a common discourse about Christ's suffering. Though I'm sure someone has, I've never known anyone to lift them out of the text and expound on them. This passage was familiar to me, but the three words squeezed in the middle suddenly appeared more massive than the rest. Like a billboard on a freeway advertising the next "not to miss" restaurant, I could not skim over them without considering their weightiness. Jesus *"endured the cross, despising the shame."* There it was. His physical suffering on the cross, as ruthless as it was, could not be compared to the shame of the cross. It was so evident to the writer that he was inspired to separate Christ's emotional shame from His physical suffering. Pause and think about it.

Jesus despises shame.

Jesus Christ publicly carried a Roman cross on the streets to a hill they called "The Skull." The writer of Hebrews tells us Jesus was able to endure the physical pain because of *"the joy that was set before Him."* God allowed Jesus to see His physical resurrection in the future. Through the years movie producers have captured Christ's physical suffering reasonably well. But I have never seen one focus on the shame He bore. Do we skim over them because we're not sure how to portray an ashamed Jesus? That's what makes these three words so important.

Jesus despises shame.

Most pictures and figurines of the crucified Christ are dumbed down and "G Rated" to make them presentable. In the days of Roman crucifixion, however, criminals were hung naked on a cross with every private part exposed. Roman whips called a cat-of-nine-tails weakened strong men as they carried the cross to their crucifixion. The pain, though devilishly brutal, was temporary. The shame Jesus felt upon His soul was another story. Jesus despised the shame. I'm glad He did because that gives us legal grounds to loathe it too.

Why would Jesus bear the cross and yet despise the shame that came as part of the journey? Perhaps the cross was a done-deal, a once-and-for-all declaration against our screw-ups called "sin." The cross proclaims, *"All have sinned and fall short of the glory of God"* (Romans 3:23). We are all offenders in one way or another. Everyone has messed up. We have all fallen at some point. Shame, on the other hand, has this bizarre ability to hang around after we acknowledge our errors to God and others. In other words, we can be forgiven and still feel the eerie fog of shame in the air.

Brené Brown, a sociologist known for her groundbreaking research on shame, says, "Guilt is a focus on behavior. Shame is a focus on self." She continues, "Guilt says, 'I did something bad.' Shame says, 'I *am* bad.'" Guilt willingly admits we've made mistakes. Shame, however, is the emotion that tells us that because of our past actions we *are* a mistake.[4]

Just ask the prostitute, the drug addict, the pornographer, the murderer or the adulterer. They know the glaring glance of the eyes that convey, "Shame on you," without uttering a word.

But it's not only the hardcore cases who feel "the look." Kids left to parent themselves in the absence of a crack-addicted father and mother deal with shame that is not theirs to bear. It's the beautifully elegant fifty-year-old woman who, in her dark moments of seclusion, still weeps over agreeing to abort her out-of-wedlock baby thirty years ago. It's the twelve-year-old daughter whose perverted father demands that she give him her body for sex before she leaves home for school in the morning. They know, all too well, the humiliating feeling of shame.

Nowhere else in the New Testament does it tell us Jesus despised anything. Here, however, the Holy Spirit slips in a fact that's gone undetected far too long.

Jesus despises shame.

DELIVERED FROM THE SHAME OF SIN

Among the countless ways Jesus suffered, He was humiliated and spit upon by an angry mob. Perhaps this is why He despised shame so much. In ancient Eastern tradition spitting upon someone was a show of disapproval, suggesting the offender had shamed them and become a mockery of their relationship. When Job's friends saw his dreadful condition, they spit upon him (Job 30:10). He had lost his wealth, his family, all his possessions, as well as the influence of his peers. They expressed their defiance to his condition by spitting on him.

In Numbers 12:14 it tells how it was customary for a father to spit in his daughter's face if she had shamed him and the family by her actions. The father would disgrace her by publicly spitting in her face. After a time of isolation from the community, the daughter could be brought back into the family. Many ancient cultures expressed shame by spitting on those who offended their honor. In some Eastern cultures it's still practiced today.

Jesus Christ not only suffered the physical pain of crucifixion on a cross but the emotional distress of shame. Matthew 27:30 records, *"Then they spat upon Him,"* and in Mark 15:19, *"Then they struck Him on the head with a reed and spat upon Him."*

When Jesus was mocked and spit on, He bore the shame of our failures, no matter how disgraceful it was. Scripture tells us, *"He was numbered with the transgressors"* (Luke 22:37). A transgressor is someone who deliberately breaks the law. In other words, a transgressor knew better but did it anyway.

Perhaps shame hangs over you because you chose to do something, knowing full well it could lead you to a difficult place in life. You pushed the limits and did it anyway. Jesus comes along and says, "Just count Me as a transgressor, like you." In other words, He is not ashamed to be identified with you, and that's how He can deliver you (and all of us) from our shame. He not only forgave the deliberate acts of sin you were guilty of committing, but He also delivered you from shame that comes from doing them.

Someone has said the two most powerful words you can say to help someone going through emotional anguish are "Me too." When you feel the fog of shame hang over you, I want you to picture the face of Jesus covered with human saliva, dripping from His forehead into His eyes. Imagine Him looking at you saying, "Me too." He knows how you feel, and that is why He despises it so much. As you have been taught to trust Christ to free you from sin's eternal consequences, you have the right to believe He gives you the courage to face and overcome the shame that looms over you.

SHAME ATTEMPTS TO DICTATE YOUR LIFE

Shame is on God's "attack and destroy" list. Chapter 4 of John's Gospel tells the story of Jesus and His disciples on their way to Galilee when they came to a fork in the road. One road led to Samaria, a city off-limits to Jews, and the other to their destination. The Samaritans were a mixed race from Jewish-Assyrian intermarriage. Their religion became a hodgepodge of Assyrian paganism and Hebrew beliefs. Therefore, Jews considered them a disgraceful lot and would not associate with them or, for that matter, even travel the road that led to Samaria. When Jesus and the twelve came to the crossroads, He sensed a "tug" drawing Him to the religiously forbidden city (John 4:4).

Coming into Samaria, it didn't take long for Him to discover His assignment. At the center of the town was Jacob's well, a place that both the Jews and Samaritans revered. Suddenly, He spots a woman alone drawing water at the hottest time of day, a time when no one else came for water. "How about a drink for a thirsty man?" I imagine Him opening the conversation, hoping to create a dialogue that might disclose His mission. In a down-to-earth way Jesus connects to the woman by merely asking for a drink of water.

> *"Then the woman of Samaria said to Him, 'How is it that you, being a Jew, ask a drink from me, a Samaritan woman?' For Jews have no dealings with Samaritans. Jesus answered her, 'If you knew the gift of God, and who it is that says to you, "Give Me a drink," you would have asked Him, and He would have given you living water.'"* (John 4:9-10).

After engaging in some small talk about water, Jesus probes deeper and hits the nerve that exposes His purpose of meeting the woman at the well.

> *"Jesus said to her, 'Go, call your husband, and come here.' The woman answered and said, 'I have no husband.' Jesus said to her, 'You have well said, "I have no husband," for you have had five husbands, and the one you now have is not your husband; in that you spoke truly'"* (John 4:16-18).

For years I heard others teach and taught myself that this woman was a "loose living, licentious lady." She married one man after the other and was currently shacking up with yet another gullible guy. We assumed Jesus' mission was to expose her adulterous and promiscuous life. But, oh, how wrong we have been! Through my research it dawned on me that women in ancient cultures and especially Jewish women could not lawfully divorce a man. A man, on the other hand, could divorce his wife at any time, for any reason (quite literally, *any* reason).

119

In ancient societies women were "property," not people. If a woman was divorced, it was because the man had divorced her. In those days, a divorced woman either lived with relatives, married another man or became a beggar. The woman Jesus met beside the well had been thrown away five times, like garbage. Her only way to survive was to live with someone, and Jesus happens to meet her while she is living with a man. If Jesus knew details about the relationship, He withheld them. And yet, like a gossipy neighbor, our distorted Westernized thinking embellishes the story by filling in the gap with our own juicy imaginations.

Jesus' assignment was not to uncover her sin but to heal her from shame. The man she was living with was not her husband, and yet there is no mention of this being an adulterous relationship. Maybe it was. We don't know. But that's not the point of the story.

Jesus' mission was to help her walk out of shame. In that culture women drew their water early in the morning to beat the heat of the day. Since the community well was the busiest place in town, she avoided people by fetching her water at the hottest time of day when no one else was around. Shame had become her demanding dictator that ordered her life.

I understand this woman's dilemma. The last place I wanted to go was Wal-mart. In our little city where I fell, Wal-mart is the place you are sure to meet someone you know. I would do my shopping during the late hours of the night at the twenty-four-hour stores when I had less chance of running into someone who knew me. The Samaritan woman went to the well at noon for the same reason I went to Wal-mart at midnight. We both rearranged our lives merely to avoid the stares of shame.

As Jesus engages the woman at the well, she begins to realize He is far different from any man she has ever met. He looked into her soul, as well as her past, and knew every detail. And yet His tone was not condemning but consoling. Jesus did not camp on her failed history but connected with her present reality. Shame always disconnects you from people. It presses you to rearrange your life so you will not run into people who have a disdain for "your kind." Strangely, the Samaritan woman felt no need to run from Jesus.

Assuming He was a prophet, she shifts the conversation to the spiritual history of the well they are standing beside. Jesus capitalizes on the opportunity and revealed something to her that we all need to know. *God wants us to be who we are, not who we or anyone thinks we should be.* In fact, *God has an attraction for the naked and real us.*

> *"But the hour is coming, and now is, when the true worshipers will worship the Father in spirit and truth; for the Father is seeking such to worship Him. God is Spirit, and those who worship Him must worship in spirit and truth"* (John 4:23-24).

I've been intrigued with these verses for many years. I suppose it's because, at my core, I am a worshipper and have always desired to be a true worshipper. But what exactly does it look like to be a true worshipper? What does it mean to worship *"in spirit and truth"*?

Another correction to my previous interpretation of this story surfaced. I understood that to *"worship in spirit"* means to worship from the affections of our heart, rather than from religious routine. To *"worship in truth,"* however, was not as clear to me. I assumed it meant the more knowledge of His Word I had the better worshipper I would be. But I was never satisfied with this explanation. When you considered the Samaritan woman's exposure to truth was brief and limited, there had to be more to it.

The Greek word interpreted *truth* means "that which is the true," as opposed to "that which is false." Digging deeper, I found it also means "to be genuine and unconcealed." In other words, to be *real—who you are.*

Jesus was saying to this shame-ridden woman, "Bring your genuine and authentic self to Me." I would say, "Bring your naked self on over here." What's so astounding is that God not only receives the naked and authentic, down-to-earth worshippers, but these are the very people He seeks out. He desires the "I am what I am" kind of folk who will come to Him just as they are.

It's no coincidence that following their conversation the woman at the well was immediately delivered from the opinions of people.

Instead of rearranging her schedule to avoid them, she ran straight into the city to share her experience with anyone and everyone who would listen. *"Come see a man who told me all that I ever did"* (John 4:29). She admits that Jesus uncovered every detail about her shameful past in front of the very people she hid from for years. Incredible courage took over this woman, and that's when God's grace took over the town. *"And many of the Samaritans of that city believed in Him because of the word of the woman who testified, 'He told me all that I ever did'"* (John 4:39).

The shame-filled woman at Jacob's well modeled the kind of person the Father esteems. Consequently, the woman at the well was no longer the "woman at the well." She became the courageous lady of Samaria telling everyone she could about a God who loved them unconditionally. Some historians believe the outbreak of the Christian faith in Samaria (see Acts 8) can be traced to this Samaritan woman whom Jesus met at Jacob's well.

THE ANTIDOTE TO SHAME

Healing from shame comes when we risk vulnerability and declare the goodness of God. Walking out of isolation is an act of faith. Shame thrives in secrecy, and the more we hide, the stronger it becomes. It will send you to the well at noon or Wal-mart at midnight when you think no one else is around. But when we come out of hiding and say, "What you see is what you get," shame loses its grip. That's when God says, "I can use someone with a testimony like yours."

So what happens to a person who takes courage and runs to tell everyone about the One who knows every minute detail of their life? The possibilities are endless. When the Samaritan woman became unashamed of her shame, the whole town was affected. *"Many of the Samaritans of that city believed in Him because of the word of the woman who testified, 'He told me all that I ever did'"* (John 4:39). The past failures shame used to "shame her" became the testimonies God used to transform a city. Amazing!

After God pressed me to come out of cover, I started two churches and began walking the streets of a drug-infested neighborhood loving and praying for people. What's more, this happened in the same city where I once did my shopping in the middle of the night because I feared to face people who might give me "the look." God seeks for "What you see is what you get" kind of people, who will courageously come out in the open and affectionately worship Him.

COMING OUT OF THE CLOSET

One day it dawned on me I could take my shame to Jesus Christ or spend the rest of my life hiding from people I allowed to hold me captive to house arrest. By this point, I hope you understand that becoming vulnerable and coming out into the open are the beginning of defeating this monster. When I walked out of the shadows of that emotional prison, I discovered this too would be tested and where else but in a grocery store.

My great escape came about a year or so after the episode I wrote about in the opening paragraphs of this chapter. Again, while shopping, I came upon an old acquaintance on aisle four. I found myself cart-to-cart and eye-to-eye with yet another former church member. The rumor mill had informed me this woman publicly and repeatedly vented her disgust over my failure.

When our eyes met, my reaction astounded me, and it did her as well. Before I could rethink my actions, instead of turning down another aisle and darting out the door as I had done numerous times before, I made a beeline for her. She was startled when I greeted her by wrapping her up in my best hug. Risking rejection, before I could stop myself, I leaped beyond the borders that had confined me for too long. When I pushed back at shame's limits, I discovered it lost its power to control me.

As I walked away from that chance meeting, I prayed for her. My prayer went something like, "God, free her to love, as You have freed me to love again. Set her free from *my sin* just as You set me free from it."

I had never prayed for someone to be free from *my sin* before. I wasn't sure I had a biblical shelf to sit that prayer on, but it felt right to pray nonetheless. Shame will not allow you to pray such a prayer for others. Instead, it keeps you as the center focus and sends you away seeking refuge for yourself.

I discovered that coming out and being vulnerable breaks the shackles that shame uses to restrict us. Had I not taken the courage to move beyond the confines of my house arrest, it's doubtful I would be celebrating my freedom today. Consequently, this lady and I are friends today. God answered the prayer I prayed for her, and she was, indeed, set free from me!

It's time for you to walk confidently out of the shadows. Your confidence is not in your performance, but in Christ alone. Don't give shame the pleasure of keeping you confined and limited. Like Peter who stepped over the sides of the boat and into the water, fasten your eyes on Jesus; then get up and get out.

Chapter Twelve

Clinging to Self-Pity

Self-pity masquerades as humility, while secretly blaming someone else for your bad breaks. The cure is to hearken to the words once spoken to a lame beggar, "Rise and walk." Then get up and do the very thing that seems impossible for you to do.

Shame has a twin. Its name is self-pity.

Like paternal twins, it's difficult to tell them apart. One plays upon the other, making it unclear as to which has greater influence. It's sure that wherever you find one, the other lurks nearby. They come as a pair, equally harmful, equally deadly.

Compared to what my life had been like previously, I secluded myself from the world I had known. I needed someone to speak into my life to help me navigate through the confusion, so I was encouraged when a friend and respected leader with an international ministry agreed to meet for lunch. And, to be honest, I had hoped that someone with influence would do something to bail me out of the mayhem I had gotten myself into.

We met at a restaurant, and typically, the smell of food was a treat. Just before I arrived, however, I sensed this meeting might have graver consequences. By the time I walked in, the smell was more nauseating than appetizing.

My failure was devastating, and I wanted someone to relieve me from the fallout of my choices. But I was wary of talking to anyone about it. I had hurt people, I admitted it. But was I so terrible that no one, even friends, could not give me a break? I never openly asked anyone, but this question occasionally paraded through my thoughts.

I can't recall the details of our conversation. What I remember is how my friend's face shifted into a more serious mode about twenty minutes into our visit.

"Bill, I have something I feel God wants me to tell you." His somber tone and eye contact from across the table made me feel as if he were looking *through me*, rather than at me.

"No one, not even God Himself, can help you until you stop pitying yourself. You want immediate deliverance from an issue that took you years to walk into. Following the Lord will demand that you stop wallowing in self-pity and start taking responsibility for your life, even if that means flipping hamburgers for a living."

I felt like a drunk driver suddenly sobered by a near head-on collision. The trump card I played to get sympathy was exposed, and he had called my hand. With one fell sweep, my friend snatched the mask of false humility off my face. God gave David a Nathan to confront him with himself, and my Nathan had arrived.

My ears were selective. Reflecting on the words I heard at the restaurant would sting for some time. The ones I replayed most were, *"pity party, take responsibility,"* and then, *"flipping hamburgers."* That last line was sobering. Would God require me, a former leader in our city, to flip burgers for a living? It turned out to be the best worst day of my life. I'm convinced that getting free from self-pity requires a "best worst day" to shock us into reality. I hope reading this is yours.

Self-pity is the drug of choice for the discouraged. In hardship the temptation to become self-centered becomes elevated. A self-centered person is a mental drifter, weighing options of what will make them happy again. Consequently, we erect a stronghold in our mind that keeps us at the center of life—*everyone's life*. This mental fortress holds us hostage as victims, relinquishing us of any responsibility for our recovery.

THE DEADLY OUTCOME OF SELF-PITY

Scripture tells the horrifying story of Cain and Abel, sons of Adam and Eve. Cain was a man of the land, making his living from the soil. At the same time, Abel was a shepherd and sheep farmer. Both men offered what they had to the Lord as their offering of worship. It was the offering that created the tension, at least in Cain. Genesis 4:3-5 tells the story.

> *"And in the process of time it came to pass that Cain brought an offering of the fruit of the ground to the Lord. Abel also brought of the firstborn of his flock and of their fat. And the Lord respected Abel and his offering, but He did not respect Cain and his offering. And Cain was very angry, and his countenance fell."*

After both men presented their offering to God, it says, *"The Lord respected Abel and his offering, but He did not respect Cain and his offering."* Resentment surfaced in Cain when he saw how God blessed Abel's offering rather than his. The Hebrew word translated "respect" could also be rendered "regard for" or "to look upon." It does not say how Cain recognized God's respect for Abel's offering over his own. Nevertheless, Abel's offering caught God's attention, and Cain knew it.

Instead of being happy for Abel because of God's pleasure upon his worship, Cain was irate with jealousy. I've often wondered what the outcome would have been had Cain questioned God about why He preferred Abel's offering. Why did God take more pleasure in it? It's possible even Abel didn't know, and, of course, he didn't live long enough to find out why. Even so, I'm convinced it wasn't God choosing Abel over Cain. Instead He accepted the offering itself. Let me explain.

Cain, a worker of the soil, offered what he had available, the fruit of his labor from the fields. Likewise, Abel, a sheep farmer, did the same. Abel gave *"the first born of his flock"* as worship to God. Unknown to either brother, sacrificing a lamb from his flock was a prophetic act of what was to come. The lamb got God's attention.

Jesus Christ was *"the Lamb of God who takes away the sin of the world"* (John 1:29). The offering of a lamb was the reason for God's pleasure in Abel's offering. Abel's sacrifice was a prophetic act of the future redemption of all humanity. It makes sense that God could do nothing else but honor such a sacrifice. Abel's offering was a prophetic statement that announced the restoration of Adam's seed. Abel's offering of a lamb foreshadowed God's decree to the serpent in Genesis 3:15: *"He shall bruise your head, and you shall bruise His heel."* The *"He"* was none other than the Lamb Himself, Jesus Christ.

Imagine how different things would have been if Cain had asked Abel, "The Lord's Presence is so powerful when you worship with your offering. Why the difference? I'm going to inquire of the Lord as to why He responds differently to you." But Cain didn't do that. Most times, neither do we. Cain felt rejected by God and jealousy toward his brother.

We are all susceptible to the snare of comparison. It's easy to become jealous of someone else's life when it appears God is blessing them more than you. In the case of failure, it's tempting to compare ourselves with others, wondering how it's possible for others to thrive while we struggle to keep our heads above water. Here's the question to consider: when it's obvious the Lord's delight is in someone else, do I choose to inquire why He is blessing them so I can enter into that blessing?

Jealousy overtook Cain, and Scripture says, *"His countenance fell."* When Cain perceived God's favor rested upon Abel's offering, he became self-absorbed and depressed. His attitude became a doorway for self-pity. The Lord tried to lead Cain away from the disaster his attitude invited.

> *"So the Lord said to Cain, 'Why are you angry? And why has your countenance fallen? If you do well, will you not be accepted? And if you do not do well, sin lies at the door. And its desire is for you, but you should rule over it'"* (Genesis 4:6-7).

Self-pity can lead to anger, bitterness and, eventually, hatred. Instead of viewing the Lord's pleasure as a family discovery, Cain took it personally and turned his feelings inward. We often overlook the sentence that reveals God's attempt to stop Cain's downward spiral. *"Its desire is for you, but you should rule over it."* Herein lies the remedy that sets us free from self-pity. *"Rule over it."*

Cain did not rule over it. Instead, it controlled him. The combination of depression, self-pity, jealousy and anger overcame his better judgment. In a momentary fit of rage, Cain killed his brother.

Like shame, self-pity feeds our need for recognition. It lures us to succumb to feelings of selfish compassion. Once absorbed into our fallen state, all that matters is that we are vindicated. The Lord told Cain, *"Its desire is for you."* Make a note of the word *it*. This word stands alone because *it* (self-pity) has a life of its own that will master us if we do not, first, master it.

The responsibility is upon us to make the first move. God never offered to do it for Cain. Instead, He told Cain to take responsibility and rule (have dominion) over his feelings.

EVEN KING DAVID

One of the most significant kings in history grew up as a shepherd and as a young adult traversed the countryside as a fugitive before finally taking the throne. Running from the deadly threats of his predecessor, King Saul, David and his fighting men lived in caves throughout the countryside of Adullam. David was a strong spirited young man with keen spiritual sensitivities. His forced, nomadic lifestyle in the rugged terrain enabled him to glean military strategies that would help develop his legacy as the king.

Thirty men, misfits to society but skilled warriors on the battlefield, joined David to champion his cause. They were known for their heroic feats, one warrior killing eight hundred men with a spear (2 Samuel 23:8). Throughout Israel, those who knew of David were confident God had anointed him to be the next king of Israel.

Even so, after years of running from Saul, David became tired and emotionally weary. Battle-fatigued and discouraged, he turned inward and surrendered to self-pity. Instead of pushing forward, David retreated to the camp of Israel's fiercest enemy, the Philistines, where he lived with them for over a year.

David took on something of a Philistine spirit, raiding and looting neighboring cities. Focusing our attention on the bad hand we have been dealt always leads to a dead end. It's impossible to rebound and fulfill our destiny when we embrace such an attitude. Even King David became vulnerable to self-pity.

THE HIDDEN AGENDA

David suppressed his thoughts and rehearsed his hardships far too much. Scripture says, *"David **said in his heart"*** (1 Samuel 27:1, bold added). "Self-talk" is a seed that impregnates our destiny. In the privacy of our minds we sketch out our roadmap for the future.

We are a display of what we think about most. Proverbs 23:7 says, *"As he thinks in his heart, so is he."* Our minds are the stage where we rehearse our future before it happens. In our minds we create a future around the bad breaks we've suffered or the breakthrough we envision. What we rehearse on the private stage of our minds eventually becomes our reality. David's retreat to the Philistine camp was a result of self-pity manifested through his negative self-talk.

Look closely at the Scripture. *"David **said in his heart**, 'Now I shall perish someday by the hand of Saul. There is nothing better for me than that I should speedily escape to the land of the Philistines'"* (1 Samuel 27:1, bold added). Nothing was further from the truth. It was not God's will David should perish by Saul's hand or retreat to the land of the Philistines. Many years ago, the prophet Samuel prophesied it was the will of God to place David on Israel's throne. In his exhausted, emotional state, however, David didn't look or feel like a king. When he compared his present reality to what the prophet anointed him to become, David yielded to self-pity. David's retreat to the Philistine camp began when he confessed and rehearsed the words of self-pity *"in his heart."*

This pitiful thinking postponed David's assignment to his God-given purpose and destiny. Being the man of courage he was, he corrected himself and rose above this low point. My hope is the same for you. You, too, can rebound as David did and move on, but you first need to choose to rule over self-pity or be ruled by it. Walking out of your own Philistine camp is up to you.

THE "RESIST LIST"

It doesn't require one to be that far along in the faith to see that self-pity is a spiritual battle. The application to win this bout, however, is conveniently practical. By engaging our natural thinking, the invisible forces of evil seduce us to turn inward and become self-centered. To counter the attack, we merely take away the thing they feed upon most, our self-centered thinking.

The most practical form of deliverance from the devil's assault is resistance. With self-pity I found resistance to be a scriptural and fruitful weapon. We're implored to submit to God and resist the devil as a means of overcoming spiritual battles.

> *"Therefore submit to God. Resist the devil and he will flee from you"* (James 4:7).

> *"Be sober, be vigilant; because your adversary the devil walks about like a roaring lion, seeking whom he may devour. Resist him"* (1 Peter 5:8-9).

The word *resist* means "oppose, stand against or give an opposite response" in a given situation. In other words, given the opportunity to fall into despair and pity, your responsibility in spiritual warfare is to *do*, *think* and *say* the opposite of what you feel.

I compiled a "Resist List" I applied to myself when I was rebounding from a fall. These will help you oppose the forces of self-pity. Keep it before you or make your own list, but do something practical to remind yourself to stay on the path.

Resist Giving Up

I'm hesitant to advise you just to go on with your life. My reluctance comes from interpreting this advice as the freedom to make another wrong decision that could lead to an even worse outcome. When it comes to being stuck in the vicious cycle of self-pity, however, I part ways with that counsel. You've lost a lot, but you are still alive, which means you have not reached your finish line. As long as you're sucking air, life is not over for you. Get up and move on with your life!

I cannot count the times I gave up. But I kept coming back. Time after time I failed, but I returned to my heavenly Father. Sitting before Him, I would pray, "Father, I know I'm not getting this right, but I know You and You alone are my hope. No matter how much I fail, I'm not leaving until, by Your grace, I get this right."

Still today, every morning, I take holy communion and sit with the Lord. Even after a bad day, with bread and cup in hand, I pray, "It's me again, Lord. I'm here because my hope is in You. I'm not here because I'm good. I've come because You're good."

Tomorrow morning get up earlier than usual, find a quiet place and worship God. Sit with Him. Pray simple prayers. Thank Him for His goodness and grace, even if you don't feel it. Ask for hope because He's the God of all hope. Choose to believe He has a good future for you because He does. In this atmosphere of worship and thanksgiving, don't dance with your feelings. Merely praise God for giving you another shot at your life and destiny. While you're there, thank Him that when you were at your worst He never left you or forsook you. He never will. You'll be amazed at how this daily routine can defuse the authority self-pity has over your life.

Resist Unforgiveness and Bitterness

Walking away from the temptation to withhold forgiveness is also an intentional decision and a daily action. This section echoes what I wrote in chapter 10, but as daunting as this is to do it bears repeating. Here's how God led me through it.

I called by name every person who came to mind that held an offense toward me. Then, as sincerely as I could, I asked God to bless them. I admit, when I prayed this out loud, it felt phony because, at that time, I *did not* want God to bless them. Remember: sometimes our prayer doesn't begin from a pure heart but in sheer obedience and faith. As we pray and obey, our heart and motives become cleansed by our act of obedience to God's Word.

> *"Bless those who curse you, do good to those who hate you, and pray for those who spitefully use you and persecute you"* (Matthew 5:44).

When you're tempted to become bitter, call the names of the people out loud in prayer. Forgive them as many times as it takes. For me, it was daily. Complete your prayer by decreeing God's blessing over them.

Recently a friend asked me what to do with the unforgiveness and bitterness he harbored against a person who stole thousands of dollars from him. I gave him this principle and read the Scripture to him. His quick reply was, "I can't do that!" My answer to him was, "Of course, you can't. But it's not that you cannot; you will not." We will, with or without feelings, obey God's Word and walk out of the fire or sit and stew in our misery.

Resist Assembling Sympathizers

Something within us longs to gather support when we are emotionally hurting. Warning! A meeting with sympathizers is a potential breeding ground for self-pity. This environment can turn into a slimy pond where mental, life-sucking mosquitoes breed and move about to infect others. Often, sympathizers are wounded, unhealed people easily attracted to people like them with similar wounds. Healed people are effective healers. On the other hand, wounded people may mean well, but they can also serve to keep the infection alive.

Self-pity craves the company of people willing to take on their offense and dine with them upon their sorrows. Most times, this occurs under the deception that their friendship offers an outlet not to "bottle up our sorrows."

Truth be known, our old nature loves a pity-party, even when it's someone else's pity we're partying over. In fact, those who join the party usually suffer from the same issues like the one they gather around. The danger is that these relationships, rooted in pity, are received as a genuine expression of God's love. Nothing is further from the truth. God's love does what's best for the person who needs healing, even if the application stings a bit at first.

The most confusing and yet the best thing the Lord did for me during the early days of my rebound was to allow my sympathizers to turn against me and leave. At the time, the pain was unbearable. It pressed me, however, to depend on God and find my consolation in Him rather than people. *"There is a friend who sticks closer than a brother"* (Proverbs 18:24). Read that proverb slowly because it's not merely a cute saying; it's the truth. By grace I discovered this kind of relationship with God.

Resist a Failure Mentality

As I have written in earlier chapters, life has been illustrated as a timeline, moving from one event to another. If we always made the right choices, I suppose we would progress quickly and arrive at our assignment much sooner. But life isn't like this, is it? We make wrong decisions and take pathways we should not take. When we realize we've gotten off track, we come back and start over where we messed up. The human experience repeats this until, it is hoped, we get it right. We move along, in and out, back and forth, but making progress nonetheless.

Moving forward insists we have a right frame of mind and attitude. We cannot despair when we make a wrong turn or choose the wrong route because this makes us vulnerable to a failure mentality. I know people who are intelligent and gifted, but they remain camped at the last place where they failed. Thus, they live their life with a mindset of failure.

Resist it. Embrace your responsibility in the failure then move forward. God permits you to start over and over and over. I've discovered God is not the God of the "second chance," but the God of the "tenth chance." Even if you're starting over for the hundredth time, do not allow your last wrong turn to prohibit you from getting up and trying again.

GET UP!

Speaking of getting up, this is an excellent way to end this chapter. God will not allow us to indulge ourselves in the murky pool of failure. Joshua realized this after he made a wrong turn and failed to lead Israel to victory against the little city of Ai. Joshua 7:7-9 tells of Israel's defeat to this small tribe. Following the embarrassing loss, Joshua falls before the Lord and prays,

> *"Alas, Lord God, why have You brought this people over the Jordan at all—to deliver us into the hand of the Amorites, to destroy us? Oh, that we had been content, and dwelt on the other side of the Jordan! O Lord, what shall I say when Israel turns its back before its enemies? For the Canaanites and all the inhabitants of the land will hear it, and surround us, and cut off our name from the earth. Then what will You do for Your great name?"*

I still smile at God's response to Joshua's prayer. Broken over his defeat at Ai, he prayed his best heartfelt prayer. After Joshua ripped his clothing and fell on his face in desperation, God's response is classic.

> *"Get up! Why do you lie thus on your face?"* (Joshua 7:10).

I've been there and done that! God would not give Joshua sympathy. The Promised Land was ahead, and Joshua could not claim it while lying on the ground in a puddle of self-pity—even *prayerful* self-pity.

It's rare for anyone to find deliverance from self-pity by committing themselves to a more in-depth devotional life. I didn't get free by praying or reading the Bible more or by being prayed over by other people. I chose to change my way of thinking, got up and walked out of it day-by-day until I stopped thinking about how bad things were for me.

Do you want to move forward? Then be courageous and *"Get up!"* That's God's Word, not mine. Self-pity is not becoming to a child of God. It's not our style, and we don't wear it well. Drop the negative talk. Stop the whining and jerk off the mask of false humility. You still have some distance to cover while getting another shot at your life and destiny. So hold on and push forward.

Chapter Thirteen

The Secret to Overcoming Discouragement

The road to a promised land always leads through a wilderness. The greatest test is not the step of faith it requires to begin but pressing on after we have started. So many journey so far and get so close, only to stop inches short of the treasure because they surrendered to discouragement.

The most profound victories come without ever striking a blow. Conquests of this nature are fought on the battlefield of the mind long before they become a hand-to-hand conflict.

Mohammad Ali—arguably, one of the greatest boxers of all time—knew how to defeat his opponents before swinging the first punch. Before the boxing match, at pre-fight interviews, Ali struck first with intimidation. As far as the media was concerned, his brilliant publicity stunts made for great marketing, increasing interest and revenue. As far as Ali was concerned, the pre-fight publicity was the first round of the boxing match.

For those privileged to watch him, the weeks leading up to the fight were as engaging as the fight itself. He provoked his opponents with words, babbling on about how he would embarrass them when they stepped into the ring. Using rhymes and belittling one-liners, Ali publicly humiliated his opponents, even predicting the round when he would knock them out. He gained the advantage with words that assaulted their mind, weeks before landing a blow to their head. After all, you cannot win a fight if you're unaware you are already in one. Mohammed Ali gained the edge of victory the moment he started talking.

DISCOURAGEMENT EXPOSED

Someone told a parable about the devil having a yard sale. As it goes, the devil put the tools of his trade on exhibition. As a shopper looked at the display, he noticed jealousy, pride, lust, envy and so on up for sale. One well-worn tool was sitting in the corner, apparently worn out from use. It was noticeably also the most expensive.

Puzzled over the price, the shopper asked the devil, "Why are you asking more for that old, rickety worn-out tool in the corner? Why, you have it priced higher than all the others you have for sale."

The devil replied, "Oh, that's because it's the most useful. I've used it more than all the others put together. When I can't get any of the other tools of my trade to work, this one always does the trick. It's the most valuable one I have. I call it *discouragement*."

Those determined to rebound from failure will find themselves in a spiritual war that's fought in the trenches of the mind. In this battle, like so many others, discouragement is the enemy's preferred weapon upon the mind. Through the medium of words, he blasts us with thoughts that weaken and tempt us to surrender. Paul warned in Ephesians 6:10, *"We do not wrestle against flesh and blood, but against. . .spiritual hosts of wickedness in the heavenly places."* Living out the Christian life requires times when we need to be embraced and warmed, and other times we need to engage and war. Either way discouragement cannot go unchallenged, for it will challenge us.

In this warfare our most vulnerable place of weakness is our five physical and mental senses. Too often, if we *feel* defeated, we presume we are. These foreboding thoughts crush hope and chip away at our confidence until we no longer recall the hope-filled words God spoke to us. Discouragement intimidates to gain a mental victory, persuading us to admit we are defeated before we even think of a battle plan. Many potential rebounders raise the white flag of surrender on the battlefield of their mind before they ever strike a blow. For them, the contest begins and ends here.

MOSES ON THE REBOUND

Before leading the children of Israel out of slavery, the first enemy God warned Moses to beware of was not Pharaoh and his army. His most elusive enemy would be discouragement.

Moses grew up as a Hebrew prince in Egypt with the dream of freeing his Hebrew countrymen from slavery. After watching an Egyptian mistreat a fellow Hebrew, Moses' zeal for his people rose up, and he killed the Egyptian. For some odd reason, the Hebrews kept a mental note of this murder. Later, when Moses stepped in to settle a tiff between two Hebrews, insisting brothers should not fight, they turned on him.

In the book of Exodus 2:14, it cites how one of the Hebrews reacted furiously and said to Moses, *"Who made you a prince and a judge over us? Do you intend to kill me as you did the Egyptian?"* Instead of Moses rallying his Hebrew brothers around him, they used the murder of the Egyptian as grounds to reject him. Moses responded by fleeing to the desert to hide. Recorded in Exodus 3, his story picks up forty years later. Now, married with children, we discover Moses working for his father-in-law, herding sheep.

After spending forty years raising a family and shepherding sheep, God visited him in a burning bush, restoring his purpose and giving him another shot at delivering his people from slavery. It took some convincing. It appears Moses had lost all confidence as a leader of people. Moses, however, finally embraced the idea that God had kept his divine purpose intact and was rebounding him to lead people rather than sheep to greener pastures. Moses' burning bush encounter with God signaled his re-entry back to God's design for his life and destiny.

Before he set out for the Promised Land, God gave Moses directives we all need as we begin our journey back to claim His promise for our lives. He instructs Moses,

> *"Look, the Lord your God has set the land before you; go up and possess it, as the Lord God of your fathers has spoken to you;* **do not fear or be discouraged***"* (Deuteronomy 1:21, bold added).

They were commanded to keep the vision of the Promised Land and God's Word before them. If they lost sight of these, they were sure to lose their way. And yet this alone would not be enough to give them success. God warned them to prepare themselves to face fear and discouragement. In fact, thousands of Hebrews died in the wilderness without inheriting God's promise because fear and despair got the best of them.

When obstacles arise, it's not always because you're out of God's will or have taken the wrong path. Discouragement can be a landmark telling you that you're spot on and heading in the right direction. When Moses determined to obey God, his battles intensified. If Pharaoh could stop him before he left Egypt, he could win without a fight. Discouragement is a mental tactic used to defeat us in the early stages of our quest to reclaim the promises of God for our lives.

The devil fiercely opposes anyone who attempts to rebound from their fall. Perhaps it reminds him of a resurrection he would rather forget. The resurrection of Jesus Christ proved to him a comeback is more detrimental to the kingdom of darkness than the original version ever was. Consequently, he fights tooth and nail to discourage us. He would prefer we remain hidden on the backside of our desert. If he can keep us "in our place" we will be one less warrior with whom he has to contend. He's fought rebounders before, and he knows they come back with greater strength and authority than they had before they fell. The warrior he fears to contend with is you.

Moses' obedience didn't mean God would remove all discouraging circumstances. In fact, opportunities to be discouraged would come from Pharaoh, the Israelites and even his own family. The pathway that leads to the promises of God can be a bumpy road with potholes of discouragement along the way. We need to remember the promise lies on the other side of obedience as we press on in the face of opposition.

DISCOURAGING VOICES

The Old Testament book of Ezra contains one of the most inspiring comeback stories found in the Bible. Because of their disobedience, Jeremiah prophesied God would discipline Israel for seventy years by allowing them to be defeated and exiled to Babylon. By the time Ezra comes on the scene, seventy years have passed, but restoration is far from complete. The book describes Ezra as a *"skilled scribe in the Law of Moses"* (Ezra 7:6). By the time he arrives in the city of Jerusalem, the city walls and the temple are still not rebuilt.

It was a miracle King Cyrus of Persia would make a decree that Israel should be allowed to rebuild the house of the Lord. He not only permitted Ezra to return to Jerusalem to begin building but also funded the rebuilding operation, restoring Israel's treasury King Nebuchadnezzar had stolen when he ruled in Babylon.

Still, under Persian and Babylonian control, the Hebrews' return to Jerusalem remains one of the great revivals of ancient Israel. Unexpected resources and a fulfilled prophecy came about through the pagan King Cyrus. Even so, rebuilding the temple of God in Jerusalem would not come about without a battle. As they began work on the temple, Scripture says,

> *"Then the people of the land tried to discourage the people of Judah. They troubled them in building, and hired counselors against them to frustrate their purpose all the days of Cyrus king of Persia, even until the reign of Darius king of Persia"* (Ezra 4:4-5).

Restoring the temple was viciously criticized by *"the people of the land."* The opposition was so fierce the Israelites soon forgot God's miraculous favor and provision. The voices of resistance frustrated the Hebrews from fulfilling their purpose, and they stopped the rebuilding project altogether. Bible scholars suggest the people delayed their work on Jerusalem for nearly twenty years. After an encouraging beginning, mere words and discouraging taunts from people *"troubled them in building."* At the first sign and sound of discouragement, God's people forsook their purpose and fled.

The devil is shrewd in how he uses people to discourage us. Discouragement can even come from God's people, persuading us to give in to despair and quit. If we're going to make progress, we'll need to ask the Holy Spirit to help us discern the difference between wise counsel and disheartening chatter. God's counsel, even in discipline, is always laced with hope. Discouragement, on the other hand, leaves us at a dead end of hopeless. In Romans 15:13, the apostle Paul called God *"the God of hope."* He walks us through discipline leaving footprints of hope in the sands of life, making us aware of the imprints of His presence upon our lives.

Twenty long years passed, and Ezra had had enough. He issued a decree to God's people.

> *"'Rise up; this matter is in your hands. We will support you, so **take courage** and do it.' So Ezra rose up and put the leading priests and Levites and all Israel under oath to do what had been suggested. And they took the oath"* (Ezra 10:4-5, bold added).

After they allowed the rant of hecklers to deplete their resolve to continue the restoration project, Ezra commands, *"Take courage."* Without courage, Ezra knew they would not finish their God-given assignment. Furthermore, he was aware that courage would not come to those who wait for it, but to those who *take it*. I have discovered courage never falls on us like an unexpected rainstorm. We have to *take courage* and make it our possession.

And how do we take our courage back? Ezra conveys this with two little words: *"do it."* They abandoned their courage and stopped rebuilding the moment they gave ear to the people's voice. To become courageous again, Ezra commanded them to *"do it"* in the face of discouraging voices and circumstances. Obedience is the language and exercise that replenishes bold faith. Raw obedience is the primer for courage.

In the kingdom of God, *doing* precedes *feeling*. Even in the natural world, advantages of physical exercise begin with moving before we feel the benefits. Likewise, we drive away discouragement by "doing" even when voices try to kidnap our emotions and deadlock our actions. In wisdom, Ezra commanded the people to *"take courage and do it."*

THE DAY DISCOURAGEMENT SHOWED UP AT CHURCH

It was a Sunday in November when our young, storefront church welcomed the largest crowd that had ever come for Sunday morning worship. God's presence was evident that day. The liberty I experienced while preaching was beyond a usual Sunday, so I looked forward to the evening service.

In the evening, the worship began with the same passion we experienced that morning. But about ten minutes into the worship time a lady who had found a home in our little church began wandering around the room praying for people. It was common knowledge she could get emotional at times. While we sang, she moved from person to person, first to those who knew her well and then to people who apparently did not. The more she prayed, the louder she got. Consequently, quite a few who didn't know her, and a few who did, headed for the exit. I wanted to leave too, but I couldn't. After all, I was the pastor.

Somehow, I was able to bring the service back to a semblance of order, and yet we lost something besides people in the transition. The lady's spontaneous praying had interrupted the beauty of God's presence. We were more aware of her than Him. My attempt at preaching was like hammering on a rock. When I looked at the people who had stayed to brave the fiasco, their riddled faces begged the question, "What just happened?"

As the evening worship service came to a close, people exited quickly, and I was left alone to lock up the building. Bewildered at what had taken place, I walked to a room behind the platform, plopped down on a chair and sank my head into my hands. "How different the morning had been from what we experienced that evening," I thought.

"How," I asked myself, "could we have a morning service so heavenly and six hours later experience something so bizarre?"

At that moment, a spirit of discouragement hit me like a sniper's bullet. Two questions uncontrollably ricocheted through my mind. First, "Would people return?"

That morning it seemed like our little church had experienced a breakthrough. I felt good about our direction and God's blessing upon the congregation.

"If our little church grew," I thought, "it would prove to our city that my repentance and restoration were genuine—that God had restored me and I had rebounded to my purpose and destiny." After that evening service I wasn't so sure.

The second question was even more lethal.

"Will God ever use me again as He once did? Will my failure hinder me from ever succeeding again?"

Before I reached home, my thoughts had set up like cement, and a dark cloud settled over me like nothing I'd ever known. Discouragement found an entryway into my heart. For a season, it stripped me of hope to regain the life and destiny God had for me.

The next Sunday my fears proved right as the crowd was much smaller and the energy level much less. Each week, like a slow leak, our momentum dissipated. I prayed as best I could for a breakthrough, but nothing came. The atmosphere in the worship services became heavy, making it difficult to lead. Discouragement had found a doorway, not only to me, but also *through me*, and the vision of our church became clouded. Meanwhile, I didn't tell anyone about the inner darkness I was experiencing, but they sensed it, nonetheless.

A couple of weeks following that disastrous Sunday evening service, while chatting with a church member, I was taken aback when he said, "For some reason, I've been terribly discouraged for the last week or so."

My attention was piqued. "You, too," I thought. But it was the next comment that sent the wake-up call.

"You know," he said, "I have no reason to be discouraged. It just dropped on me out of nowhere."

I knew what had happened. I was the doorway of my friend's discouragement. Slowly, it began to wrap its tentacles around the minds of people in our church. An anointing, whether it's from God or the devil, flows from the one in authority to those under authority. This evil anointing of discouragement had found a place in me and was now settling upon the church under my charge. I had permitted it, and it would be my responsibility to break its hold.

THE SECRET DISCOVERED

The following day I set myself to seek God for an answer. I searched the Scriptures, looking up the word *discourage* in its various forms. In short time, the Holy Spirit revealed to me the answer. In fact, I gave you the answer at the beginning of this chapter, in Deuteronomy 1:21.

> *"Look, the Lord your God has set the land before you; go up and possess it, as the Lord God of your fathers has spoken to you; **do not fear or be discouraged"** (bold added).*

There it was, hidden in plain sight for kings who would give themselves to search it out. Proverbs 25:2 reminds us, *"It is the glory of God to conceal a matter, but the glory of kings to search out a matter."* Admittedly, this was not what I wanted to find. I was hoping for something like a formula that required much less responsibility on my part. Nonetheless, here it was, the secret God gave Moses to face his discouragement is also the one we will use to overcome ours.

Do not fear or be discouraged.

God never promised to remove discouraging circumstances from Moses as he led Israel from Egyptian slavery. On the contrary, He warned him they would arise. The command *"Do not fear or be discouraged"* is the clue that warned Moses of impending discouragement as he took his journey toward the promise of God. In fact, many of the Hebrew people who left Egypt with him would never make it to the Promised Land because they let go of courage when faced with opposition. God's plan to keep Moses free from discouragement was in His Word. But it would require something from Moses because the secret was the command itself.

Freedom from discouragement does not come by experiencing cheerful events that overshadow the negative ones. Certainly, encouragement can drive away despair, but we don't live on a mountaintop where outside resources always supply ample doses of support. In this case, we become dependent upon whatever or whoever makes us consistently happy. In this pharmaceutical age we seek for a "happy pill" rather than following God's given strategy.

God never instructed Moses to overcome discouragement through long seasons of prayer, though he spent weeks and months at a time alone in God's presence. His plan to free Moses from discouraging situations would be through raw, gutsy obedience to His Word.

The secret was in the command, *"Do not be."*

Later, when Joshua replaced Moses as Israel's leader, the same charge was given to him before he faced his own discouraging battles. I'm sure Joshua had gleaned wisdom from watching his predecessor, Moses, as he met various situations in the wilderness. One could argue that discouragement kept the elder leader from entering the Promised Land. When the children of Israel grumbled yet again for lack of water, in anger Moses struck the rock rather than speak to it as God commanded (see Numbers 20:8-12). Discouragement is expressed in various ways, even, and maybe especially, through anger. And so God instructs Joshua with similar words.

> *"Be strong and of good courage. . . . Only be strong and very courageous, that you may observe to do according to all the law which Moses my servant commanded you. . . . Have I not commanded you? Be strong and of good courage; do not be afraid, nor be dismayed, for the Lord your God is with you wherever you go"* (Joshua 1:6-7, 9).

146

Consider David, as he and his warriors approached the city of Ziklag where they lived while dwelling in the land of the Philistines. Returning from a mission, they found the town burned with fire, and their wives and children were taken captive by the Amalekites. First Samuel 30:4 tells us, *"David and the people who were with him lifted up their voices and wept, until they had no more power to weep."* Their grief was so overwhelming that David's men blamed him and wanted to kill him. The men who had been his encouragers turned on him, and David was left alone in his distress. Even so, David knew the secret. Scripture tells us, *"David encouraged himself in the Lord his God"* (1 Samuel 30:6, KJV).

God did not remove the grim circumstances for Moses, Joshua or David. Neither will He remove all of ours. Deliverance begins with the choice to stay focused on the word God gave us in fulfilling His purposes in our lives. The Lord's command to Moses and Joshua was not mere motivational rhetoric or a self-help affirmation, but a word from God.

Jesus warned His disciples about the discouragement they would face as they approached His crucifixion. As their mission appeared to be unraveling and losing momentum, John 14:1 records Christ's words to His disciples. *"Let **not** your heart be troubled; you **believe** in God, **believe** also in Me"* (bold added). Facing the most depressing time of their lives, His crucifixion, Jesus gave His disciples the antidote for discouragement. *"Let not. . .believe,"* was the secret. In other words, "don't let yourselves be controlled by what you see and feel. Stay the course."

In my quest to find the secret to break the power of discouragement, I came to realize I was drawing my inspiration from outside sources, increased church attendance and people's positive response to my sermons. I tried to validate my rebound to purpose and destiny by outward success. On a Sunday night when this evaporated I became lost to the shadowy world of discouragement. God was not the source of my despair. He never is. After all, He's the one who gives the promise to restore purpose and destiny. When I applied the command I discovered in God's Word I changed, and then the atmosphere of the church changed.

When we stop waiting for an event (like winning the lottery) to boost us out of discouragement, the sooner the fog will lift. Eating the fruit someone else planted in the Promised Land is easy, but ariving there will require obedience, faith and patience. It's a given that opportunities will arise to stop us. The secret to overcoming discouragement comes in the form of raw obedience to God's command to believe and keep walking.

Do not be discouraged!

Chapter Fourteen

Restoring Relationships

If the Bethlehem story of Christ's birth is anything, it's God saying He will live with animal dung, slobbery feeding troughs and sweaty shepherds just to be near us. When we find ourselves in messy and foul places, God unexpectedly shows up and says, "I love you."

God frames His kingdom around relationships. He gave Moses ten commandments to guide Israel in their daily life. Four of the ten instruct us in our relationship with Him. Surprisingly, the remaining six speak of our connection with people. All ten guide us in God's way of doing life, but it's interesting that God's greater emphasis was on our relationship with one another.

Regardless of whether human relationships immediately resume as they were before we fell, it's essential we take steps to heal the rifts that resulted from our trouble. It's a sign we are getting up from our fall when relationships with people involved with and affected by our situation begin to heal. Some will recover quickly, while others will take years. In either case, as we rebound from the troubled times in our lives, the way back to fulfilling our purpose and destiny should lead us down a path to restore wounded relationships.

Hundreds, possibly thousands, of people in my city were affected by the choices I made that caused my failure. The day I stopped blaming others and took responsibility for my actions was when I began asking God to whom I should make amends.

What a discovery this was! I found perplexed people—some mad, others sad, but mostly confused—trying to make sense out of my choices that caused my fall. It was impossible for me to go to everyone, so I asked God whom He wanted me to approach. The people I had lived life with for more than twenty years needed closure. As for me, I wanted to know I had done everything I was supposed to do to help them bridge the gap from anger to love, confusion to comfort, and sadness to serenity.

In the beginning, my willingness to approach people was pretty selfish. I did it for myself. I simply could not face myself and move on without first facing them. I wasn't sure who would remain part of my world, but I knew I couldn't live with myself without, first, facing whomever I felt God was leading me to approach. And so, meet them I did. I prayed for guidance that He would bring to mind the names of people I needed to contact. One by one, as names and faces popped onto my mental screen, I would call and set up a meeting. Over more cups of coffee than I care to count, I confessed my shortcomings and asked for their forgiveness.

Did these meetings fully restore relationships and allow me to proceed with life as though nothing happened? No. Not immediately and even then, not with everyone. To this day, however, I am grateful for how God continues to reconnect me with people who became estranged from me because of my failure. Now, years later, people still walk back into our lives. I've discovered fruit produced from rebounding ripens slowly. Because we're part of a relational kingdom, people connected to our lives are as much a part of our comeback as we are. And, as with all things in God's kingdom, it's worth waiting on.

Our primary concern is to find reconciliation to God and the people in our lives that matter most. As we obey the Lord, a natural flow will recover lost positions and opportunities. Our priority, however, should never be to regain lost positions merely but repair hurt relationships. Never forget this: *people are the objects of God's love.* God has two chief aims for us. The first is to restore an intimate relationship with Him. His second priority is to reconcile us to the people closest to us who were affected by our failure.

CRACKS IN OUR FOUNDATION

With profound compassion and love, our Father is eager for us to discover a deeper intimacy with Him than we've ever known. Many assume that since they didn't change religions they remain connected to Him. Indeed, God promised never to leave or forsake us (Hebrews 13:5). Even so, in our disappointment with ourselves, most of us walk away from our nearness with God. It's as if we still have the family name but never come home to visit. Prayer, Scripture reading and personal worship cease to be part of our daily routine. We still believe (at least, mentally) that having personal time with our heavenly Father is essential, but we no longer spend time alone with Him in the secret place. We're still in the family, but our hearts have become captive to a far country and relationship is broken. More than forgiving our sin, the Holy Spirit moves us to repair fractures in the foundations of our lives that support our relationship with God.

I assure you, this collapse didn't happen all at once. It took place slowly, over time. Like fractures that occur in the foundation of a building, the public eye doesn't notice them. Outwardly we may appear stable and strong, but we know brokenness is there, hidden from the surface. In time, the foundation of our faith becomes compromised, and the structure of our life becomes shaky. Now the cracks, no longer hidden, become public and our character tarnished. If sin caused the failure, your relationship with God was vulnerable long before the break in the foundation became public.

INTIMACY WITH GOD RESTORED

Once again, consider how God dealt with Jacob. Years after Jacob conned his brother, Esau, out of his birthright, the time came when he was forced to restore their relationship. Jacob feared his brother because after he swindled him out of the inheritance Esau wanted to kill him. Genesis 31:3 says, *"Then the Lord said to Jacob, 'Return to the land of your fathers and to your family, and I will be with you.'"*

Before Jacob could reconcile with his brother and family, however, he would be led to a place where his broken intimacy with God would heal. For this to happen, God led Jacob back to the familiar place called Bethel. Jacob, however, still feared meeting Esau more than meeting God. Fearing a confrontation with Esau, Jacob prayed,

> *"O God of my father Abraham and God of my father Isaac, the Lord who said to me, 'Return to your country and to your family, and I will deal well with you': Deliver me, I pray, from the hand of my brother, from the hand of Esau; for I fear him, lest he come and attack me and the mother with the children"* (Genesis 32:9, 11).

God answered Jacob's prayer and delivered him from the wrath of Esau, but Jacob would not be allowed to sidestep his confrontation with God Himself. God loved Jacob too much to let him go. Before Jacob would have an eye-to-eye meeting with Esau, he would first tussle with God face-to-face. Unaware of what was ahead, Jacob was about to have a head-on collision with the Almighty. This encounter would have a lasting effect that would not soon be forgotten.

As Jacob journeyed toward his homeland, the looming confrontation with Esau drew near. To soften Esau, while his family camped on the opposite side of the Jabbok, Jacob sent a servant ahead bearing gifts for his estranged brother. Scripture records,

> *"So the present went on over before him, but he himself lodged that night in the camp. And he arose that night and took his two wives, his two female servants, and his eleven sons, and crossed over the ford of Jabbok. He took them, sent them over the brook, and sent over what he had. Then Jacob was left alone; and a Man wrestled with him until the breaking of day"* (Genesis 32:21-24).

Finally, Jacob was in a position where God could deal with him. Jacob was *alone*.

Coming back into an intimate relationship with God is a priority over all others, and God takes it seriously. In fact, we cannot adequately return to our purpose and destiny or a relationship with other people until we have courageously returned to God. A fresh encounter with God prepares us for the meeting that restores us to people. We come away from God broken, which postures us to be received by others.

Just as God was calling Jacob back to intimacy with Himself before his meeting with Esau, He will lead you through the same pattern. Jacob's greatest rebound was not to his brother, but to the God of his fathers. Once this happens, everything else can fall into proper order.

Do you feel alone? If so, it could be that the Lord is putting a "Jacob move" on you. After all, our relationship with God began alone, and this is still where He deals with us best. I suppose this is why we refer to our relationship with Jesus as a "personal relationship." Alone with God, in private chambers, the heart and soul of our getting up from our fall are consummated as we rebound to the life and destiny He's given us.

While alone, the Lord appeared to Jacob in the form of a man. Theologians call these heavenly experiences a *Theophany*, which refers to moments in history when God revealed the Christ to people on earth before His physical birth in Bethlehem.

Jacob *"wrestled with him until the breaking of day."* It's interesting that the word in the original Hebrew text rendered "wrestled" also means "dirt" or "dust." When God created man, Genesis 2:7 says He formed us from *"the dust of the ground."* The implication is that God reduced Jacob back to man's most humble state, mere *"dust."* It's here God can reshape us into the image He imagined for us all along. We become like moldable clay in the hands of the Master Potter.

Before Jacob's wrestling was over, he would experience yet another new beginning with the Father, a first love relationship of sorts. Hebrews 10:32 exhorts us to *"think back on those early days when you first learned about Christ"* (NLT). The Lord desires to restore our relationship with Him as it was before our fall. To do this, God reduces us to dust, which serves to make us pliable and moldable in the hands of a loving Father. During the intense wrestling Jacob's strength left him, and finally God had him where He wanted him. When nothing was left in Jacob, God could mold him into His image and fulfill his destined assignment.

You may feel as if you're in a hand-to-hand grapple with people, problems or the devil himself. More than likely, it is God who contends with you. Do not despair. Though this may be the most vulnerable place you've ever been in, it's also the best place you could be. You are in a "God place." You are at a purer, more basic form of existence, much like the one God began with when He formed Adam from the dust of the earth. From your vulnerable place God is molding you into His masterpiece, the image of purpose and destiny you are called to fulfill.

Jacob thought his battle was with Esau. Perhaps we all feel this way when we find ourselves so defenseless. We assume our struggle is with people. In the early stages of rising from a fall, getting up can feel so complicated because we are wrestling with God. These battles are meant to diminish your strength in yourself so God can move you to draw from His strength and power. These are days of utter dependence upon God's ability to bring you into deep intimacy with Himself.

CHERISH YOUR LIMP

Some physiologists say the hip is the stoutest part of the human anatomy. If this is true, Jacob became disabled at his strongest point. As if returning to his base form of "dust" wasn't enough, *"Jacob's hip was out of joint as He wrestled with him"* (Genesis 32:25). The ablest part of Jacob became crippled during his confrontation with almighty God. When the strength of our pride can no longer carry us, then we're positioned for our most intimate moments with the God who overpowers us with His love. Jacob's greatest blessing came when he held on tightly to God at his most vulnerable time in life.

During the late hours of the night, it dawned on Jacob he was not wrestling with a man, but with God Himself. At this revelation, Jacob makes one of the oddest statements anyone ever made to God.

"I will not let You go unless You bless me!" (Genesis 32:26). After this prayer, Jacob would not walk away in strength but limp away in weakness. For the remainder of his life, the thing that marked Jacob's encounter with God would be, *"He limped on his hip"* (Genesis 32:31). His experience with God did not reflect itself in strength but in an apparent crippling weakness. God did, indeed, answer Jacob's prayer to bless him. The blessing, however, appeared in weakness, not strength.

Too often, we want to reappear from our secret place with God, strutting with confidence. I suppose there's something within us, possibly our pride, that wants to emerge from our prayer closet with a spring in our step after a private encounter with the Holy One. Jacob's meeting, as it goes with all genuine experiences with God, left him markedly weaker—more noticeably human than ever. To this day, the traits of Jacob we speak of most are his deceitfulness and his limp. What's more astounding, Jacob was more highly esteemed *limping* away from God than he was when he *ran away* from Esau. Any strength he would now exude would be a testimony that he had had an encounter with the living God.

I wanted to hide my limp, but the only way I could do this was to leave town and relocate among people who didn't know my story. Whenever I would go to another city, my shoulders squared up, and my gait became steady. I felt more like my old, confident self. Then I would return home to live among the people who knew me best, and, once again, I shuffled along. Trying numerous times to find employment in another city, I pleaded with God to send me far away. One day, God broke His silence to me on this matter and said, "I'm going to restore you in front of those who know you best. I want to rewrite your story right before them." And so my rebound occurred at the very place where I missed my shot in life. After appearing to be knocked out, people looked on as I clawed myself up from the ground and stood up to fight again. And fight, I do, and yet my weakness remains. I now walk with a limp.

I thought my rebound was for me alone. As it turns out, it is for you, and others like you, to point you to a pathway so you too can rise to fulfill your purpose and destiny.

Friend, don't be ashamed of your limp. Those who know you best will recognize it. In time, having the courage to hobble along will become the admiration of your faith. People who know where your limp came from will admire you for having wrestled your way back into a more profound walk with God. Don't give up until your experience has forever marked you as one who would not let God go until He blessed you.

My limp, rather than evidence of my failure, has become a sign of God's restored favor and love. "Wasn't he the guy who. . .?" they ask. Reduced to dust, the Almighty revealed Himself to me in ways I had never known in my pre-limping days. Today His goodness so overshadows my weakness I hardly notice I limp. It's become an extension of who I am since wrestling with God. Now, if I happen to catch someone staring at my limp, I'm hardly aware they're looking. I simply imagine them saying, "He limps, and yet he walks on."

RESTORED TO CRUCIAL PEOPLE

The second relationship to give attention to is our relationship with the crucial people in our lives. I use the word "crucial" instead of "important" because many important people cross our path, but crucial people are those in our intimate circle. Important people include meaningful friendships that vary with circumstances. We work with them, go to the gym with them and do business with them. They come and go without much fuss or disturbance to our daily routine.

On the other hand, people who are crucial to our lives are constant. They are God-ordained and essential to our well-being. To lose a relationship with an important person does not tear at the soul as it does with someone crucial to our lives. Important people can be replaced, usually (though not always) without violating our values of life. God gives necessary instructions, however, on how to live life with crucial relationships.

Who is crucial? It starts with those nearest to us like our spouse, children and family. These relationships are in our smallest circle. Scripture speaks about the priority of spouse and children more than any other earthly ties. Indeed, a spouse is the most crucial of all human relationships for there's no other human being on earth with whom we can become "one flesh."

Pain that comes from our failure can run deep within a spouse because they often carry the guilt of the one who fell. If sin was involved, they might feel as though they are guilty of the same offense. Because of their "oneness," they too are often treated as an offender. As the person who experienced the failure walks through the wilderness experience of rebounding, the spouse will make the same journey every step of the way.

A personal friend who happens to be a pastor, due to a split in his church, suffered an emotional breakdown. The elders in his congregation rose up against him, and within months he was without financial support. The incident drove him into severe depression. His wife watched her husband become a shadow of the man she knew him to be. His weaknesses resulted in her also experiencing depression. His emotional failure became her experience, as well. This couple needed to be healed from the incident before they could return to a place of usefulness. Gratefully, they recovered, and their story ended happily. They are now fulfilling the purpose God intended, leading another church and impacting lives.

If your failure involved immorality, the pain families suffer can sometimes take years to heal. It is a more excellent testimony to God's glory when a husband and wife's relationship recovers after a fall. Such a restoration is a beautiful picture of God's redemption.

The Lord states His feelings about divorce in Malachi 2:16: *"'I hate divorce,' says the Lord God of Israel."* While the Lord hates divorce, Scripture also reveals that even God divorced Israel because of her spiritual adultery. Referring to this, Jeremiah 3:8 states, *"Then I saw that for all the causes for which backsliding Israel had committed adultery, I had put her away and given her a certificate of divorce."*

We are all uniquely created under diverse circumstances. Consequently, everyone's rebound is different. Things differ from person to person, and it's impossible for everyone to know the whole emotional rollercoaster behind a person's failure. Some relationships do not work out perfectly with the crucial people in our lives. To presume upon God's grace while practicing sin in a deceived lifestyle is not God's best, either. Scripture advises, *"Work out your own salvation with fear and trembling"* (Philippians 2:2). Compromising God's principles, however, almost assuredly prolongs our rebound.

The way you manage yourself as you return to the Lord and the crucial people in your life will determine the manner and time in which you come back to your purpose and destiny. The person who does everything possible to restore himself to his spouse and children, as well as helping them recover from the impact of the fall, will come back sooner. If failure caused a separation in your marriage, restoration would be more difficult, but not impossible, for *"with God all things are possible"* (Matthew 19:26). God's best is to seek restoration and to *"follow peace with all men"* (Hebrews 12:14), especially with your relationships that are crucial in your life. It's merely how God intended for life to work best.

Not Everyone Will Have Faith in Your Rebound

Will all your relationships be restored? I hope so, but realistically, some may not. Pray and work especially hard on the crucial ones, but don't be surprised if important relationships you had for years don't remain the same. As I pointed out, our actions impact the lives of many people. There's no way to address this subject without being honest about the effect we have on the people in our inner circle. After my failure, I lost relationships I could never imagine not being in my life. Some losses with crucial people were due to my poor choices. Others were circumstantial as they come with the territory of a fall.

Don't be surprised if you don't rebound into good standing with all of your relationships. Some people will not be able to overcome the disappointment of your failure. Simply put, they had more faith in the strength of your humanity than they should have. But we all do this to one degree or another. So don't be so hard on them for leaning on you in this way.

Furthermore, our culture and society are busy and getting busier as time progresses. Many people just will not or cannot change their routine in life to invest the time it takes to mend the disappointment your fall caused. Don't take it personally. Move on with the people who want to invest in who you are and who you are becoming.

So what do you do with people who refuse to acknowledge you are taking steps to rebound to faith and purpose? *Let them go.* That relationship may return later; but for now release them and move on with God and the people who have been given grace to walk this journey with you. As you wholeheartedly pursue God, other fulfilling relationships will show up and come alongside you as you return to fulfill your purpose.

For several years my progress was stalled over and over as I attempted to rebound to my God-ordained purpose and destiny. I wanted the same people who had been part of my life in the past to acknowledge my return and celebrate my new beginning. Unrealistically, I assumed this was what a rebound looked like. Their rejection caused me a lot of heartaches. I asked God about this, and He gave me a distinct word which helped me move on. God said, *"Not everyone has faith to believe in a resurrection."* Did you get that?

Not everyone believed Jesus resurrected from the dead. Neither does everyone today believe in His resurrection. But his closest companions believed because they saw Him alive again. They talked to Him and ate with the resurrected Christ.

So who are we to get our feathers ruffled if people, even people we were once close to, do not believe in ours? Some will believe. And they will talk with us and eat with us and do life with us.

If I waited until everyone had faith to see me rebound to my place in life, I would still be waiting. The Lord's words broke a spiritual chain that tethered me to people who did not believe God would give me the grace to get up from my fall. *Everyone who walked with me in the past was not supposed to make the trip with me into my future.* It was a painful, but necessary, lesson. If I was going to move on, I had to release them. Otherwise, the sorrow I experienced from their rejection would have halted my progress altogether.

159

I learned a lot from my mistakes. This book gives you the opportunity to learn at my expense. Welcome the humility that comes with your limp. Your brokenness is your opportunity to receive greater grace. *"God gives grace to the humble"* (James 4:6, 1 Peter 5:5).

Take my advice and do everything you can to seek reconciliation with the crucial relationships in your life. If it is impossible to find restoration with them, or if they refuse to reconcile, then move on. Live with the assurance that you are passionately pursuing Jesus and seeking His best for your life.

Chapter Fifteen

Learning, Lauding and Leaving the Past

It makes no sense to keep on stumbling over something that is behind you. Move on!

History is perhaps the most valuable information we can access. A study of the past can teach us what does and does not work. It may come as a surprise that we build the road into our future with experiences from our past. New beginnings often spring from old happenings, and this may be the golden nugget of history.

Referring to Israel's history, the apostle Paul wrote in Romans 15:4, *"For whatever things were written before were written for our learning."* He explained that the actions of Israel are fixed, forever set in time, and yet far from wasted. History rests in the past, waiting for someone to make their discovery and learn from it. Our history, the good and bad, is rich with wisdom for our future. Regardless of how brilliant or horrible, extraordinary or average, we cannot change our past, but we can use it to improve our future.

When we look at our history, we can allow it to hinder our progress or permit it to become a launching pad to run the next leg of our race. Consequently, the more we view our failures as a liability, the more inclined we are to allow them to deprive us of the successful future God has for us. Our past failures have the staggering ability either to immobilize us or to motivate us. It's our choice as to which one prevails.

I came across an old photo of myself taken in the '80s. A photographer froze my suit and hairstyle in a time warp. Glaring at the picture, I was able to pull that moment from history into the present. As I stared at it, I could feel and smell the old school room where the photographer had set up his backdrop. The voices of people in the room echoed in my mind. Even the photographer's face reappeared in my thoughts. Then my thoughts shifted from there to the house I was living in at the time, and on and on it went. Gaping at the forty-year-old photo was like opening a time capsule. It's true that whatever we focus our minds on, we become.

When you fix your thoughts on past failures, you recreate them and bring them into your present to relive over and over. Like my forty-year-old photo, history can be resurrected and freeze you in time when you focus on it. Sadly, what you were, whether right or wrong, is not who you are or who you are meant to become. By reading this chapter, my prayer is that you will look at your history and use it as a building block. The account of our history was never meant to define us indefinitely. Instead, we can glean wisdom from the past that propels us into our destiny.

LOOKING HONESTLY AT YOUR PAST

As we approach the last chapters of this book, I hope you are accepting the fact that you have to face your failure head-on. What caused you to stumble? What took place? Immorality? Divorce? Addiction? Financial collapse? Embezzlement? Did you have a misunderstanding with family or employer? Broken relationships? Were you lied about or caught in a lie? Mental illness?

What was it?

Whatever it was that tripped you up, be daring and courageous, and call it what it is. Most likely it has a name. The name, by the way, is not what you were and is certainly not what you are. Remaining vague, however, allows whatever it was to go unchallenged.

The point? You cannot be set free from what you will not admit or recognize. Not acknowledging the failure is like trying to unlock a door with the wrong key. You may argue you have a key, and, indeed, you may have a key in your possession. But if the key you have will not unlock the door that imprisons you, you remain confined. Speaking the truth about your situation is the key that opens the door that imprisons you to your past. Jesus called it *"the truth that sets you free"* (John 8:32).

As the apostle Paul revealed, history has fixed the good and bad in time. In wisdom, he notes that it's *"for our learning."* Even our failures have value when we learn something from them. The wonder of it is, I not only learn from my history, but I can also learn from yours, and you from mine.

The first key to overcoming is to look directly at your past—the pain, the mess and the people involved—and allow truth to do its work. Own it—*all of it*. That failure belongs to you. You may not have caused it, or maybe you did. Either way it's yours. Regardless, look at it and say, "That's my history."

Now what have you learned? What are you learning? Finding the lessons in it redeems it from being a black hole in your past that holds you captive to painful memories. Are you learning to forgive more fully? Are you learning you are not exempt from the consequences of wrong choices? Have you discovered the grass isn't greener on the other side? What? You have to find the lessons, and *there are* lessons to be found.

Now invite the Holy Spirit, the Spirit of truth, to come and reveal God's viewpoint to you. The Holy Spirit brings light to any situation. He is always blatantly honest and yet mercifully redeeming. When the Spirit shines His light on dark places in your past, it not only uncovers the darkness of your fall and failure but also reveals the gold buried in the ruins. *You will discover the most valuable resources to be used in your future sit in the shadows of your failure.*

I agree this can be a painful process, but don't waste a moment of it. You can trust God to help you face the pain because He doesn't want you to look at it forever. Again, remember the story of the prodigal son in Luke's Gospel. After he turned to go home, his father ran to meet him and wouldn't allow him to bring up or rehearse his past failure. In fact, the father immediately turned the conversation to his son's future, introducing to him a robe, a ring, shoes of sonship and a celebration for his return.

GREAT PEOPLE WHO FAILED

To help you face your past, consider the heroes of the Bible who had histories laced with trouble and failure. Abraham, for example, lied about his wife. Because Sarah was so beautiful, he told the Egyptians his wife was his sister. Abraham reasoned with Sarah, "If they know you're my wife, they will kill me and let you live." So, to save his hide, he lied and said, "She's my sister," which was a half-truth because Sarah was the daughter of his father, but not his mother.

They took Sarah to Pharaoh's house, another way of saying, "to his harem." Imagine allowing your wife to sleep with another man for the evening to save your own neck!

At any length, Genesis 12:16 says, *"They treated Abram well for her sake."* A man giving his wife to another man hardly resembles the father of faith we celebrate. But here he is, warts and all, recorded in the annals of history for us to read. Later, Abraham goes on to become the father of faith we all know, but not without some poor and, I might add, "stupid" decisions along the way.

Consider Moses, himself a killer, rebounded from a forty-year-old murder rap to lead the children of Israel out of Egyptian slavery.

King David's past included adultery and murder. He conspired to kill his military captain, Uriah, to cover for his adulterous fling with Uriah's wife, Bathsheba, who, by the way, became pregnant from their rooftop affair.

Our Bible heroes have nothing on modern-day soap operas. Even with a storied past like David's, Luke records in the book of Acts that he was known as a man after God's heart (Acts 13:22).

Peter, the disciple who denied even being an acquaintance, much less a close friend and disciple of Jesus, preached a sermon on the day of Pentecost (see Acts 2) that led to three thousand people following the way of Jesus.

Paul, who persecuted and conspired to murder many Christians, later penned most of the Scripture we know today as the New Testament.

In fact, if we tore out the pages of the Bible that were written or inspired by men with a record of murder, adultery or theft, Genesis through Deuteronomy (written by Moses) would be gone. Thirteen books written by Paul (fourteen if you include Hebrews) would vanish from the New Testament. Our heroes were far from perfect people.

The failed histories of these great men of God inspire me. They faced it, owned it and, through the power of God's forgiveness and rebounding grace, released it. Rather than holding them back, the past served as a launching pad that would catapult them into their future to reflect God's redeeming glory.

FACE THE PAIN

When you confront the failures in your past, you will come face-to-face with the agony you caused your family, friends and yourself. So how do you go about walking through this historic minefield without feeling the anguish of guilt?

Actually, you can't. Furthermore, you're not supposed to.

Guilt is not bad. Guilt is a signal that alerts our hearts that we have unresolved issues. As I write in chapter 11, shame tells us our past is who we are and thus unresolvable. Guilt screams to be resolved and fixed, repaired and forgiven.

So. . .*feel the pain.*

Admit your guilt. Admit *all* of it.

And don't forget the lessons. Learn all you can, and after you have learned what you need to (no option here), *let it go.*

Let *all* of it go.

God has forgiven you if you have asked Him to. Accept His forgiveness. Where necessary, ask others to forgive you.

Then forgive yourself. Completely.

Can you imagine what the outcome would have been if Peter had never forgiven himself for turning chicken and denying Jesus?

He dug deep into his soul, forgave himself for what he did and went on to affect the world in such a way we have never gotten over it.

But what if. . .just what if. . .he had not.

On the other hand, as I pointed out in an earlier chapter, Judas didn't let it go. He too was a traitor and denied the Lord, but he couldn't get over the guilt and shame. He didn't believe God would forgive him. If Judas could have held on a little longer, he would have witnessed the ultimate act of mercy, the death of Jesus on the cross and His resurrection from the grave. To escape the pain of his past, Judas killed himself. You may disagree, but I don't think he had to do what he did. Judas, like so many, gave up because he didn't know Jesus died and rose again to forgive guilty people like us.

LETTING GO

God never uses our mistakes against us. Instead, He uses even our failures to move us forward. The apostle Paul wrote,

> *"Brethren, I do not count myself to have appre-*
> *hended; but one thing I do, forgetting those things*
> *which are behind and reaching forward to those*
> *things which are ahead, I press toward the goal for*
> *the prize of the upward call of God in Christ Jesus"*
> (Philippians 3:13-14).

Never forget that this was the same man who conspired to imprison and murder Christians before he encountered Jesus on the road to Damascus (see Acts 9). Following his conversion, he lived a life filled with mistreatment and imprisonment. If Paul had not let go of his past, I'm convinced he could have become a cynical and bitter man. Naturally speaking, Paul lived a much more comfortable life *before* he committed his life to follow the Nazarene.

Paul realized that moving into his future meant letting go of all that was behind him, the good and the bad, his successes and his failures. That didn't mean he wouldn't occasionally refer to his history. Someone said that looking into our past is like driving

an automobile. As we mov␣
of our attention should be on th␣
on what's around us, however, we s␣
mirror occasionally. I emphasize *glance*, ␣

We often get into trouble when we take ␣
fixated on past failures or successes. If you try to ␣
looking back, you will steer yourself into a ditch every ␣

Jesus warned about trying to live life this way.

> *"Now it happened as they journeyed on the road, that someone said to Him, 'Lord, I will follow You wherever You go.' And Jesus said to him, 'Foxes have holes and birds of the air have nests, but the Son of Man has nowhere to lay His head.' Then He said to another, 'Follow Me.' But he said, 'Lord, let me first go and bury my father.' Jesus said to him, 'Let the dead bury their own dead, but you go and preach the kingdom of God.' And another also said, 'Lord, I will follow You, but let me first go and bid them farewell who are at my house.' But Jesus said to him, 'No one, having put his hand to the plow, and looking back, is fit for the kingdom of God'"* (Luke 9:57-62).

How often have we said, *"Lord, I will follow You wherever You go,"* only to slip back because people, practices and issues in our past still have a grasp on us?

In Luke's story, with much enthusiasm, the first man came to Jesus but wanted to stay home until his father died. In the same way, the second fellow wished to return to bid his family and friends farewell. We know what a trap this can be. As soon as we go home and tell them of our pursuit to follow Jesus, they talk us out of it.

Jesus follows these examples with a sobering statement. *"No one, having put his hand to the plow, and looking back, is fit for the kingdom of God."* The word *look* can also be rendered "meditate." Jesus implied it's impossible to contemplate or meditate on what's behind us and also move forward to what's before us. The reason? Like a puzzle piece, you cannot push it into a place where it does not *fit* and expect to create a perfect picture. Your past doesn't always match the picture God is painting today for tomorrow. It's possible to be so aware of the significance of today and the possibilities of tomorrow that we no longer need to rehash the events of yesterday. The details of yesterday, while not wasted, will not *fit* into the masterpiece God is creating from you today.

Letting Go of Past Success

Paul's statement to the church in Philippi, *"forgetting those things which are behind,"* carries profound meaning. It's true that Paul, before his conversion, persecuted Christians. He was also a successful Jewish leader, the up-and-coming golden boy of the Pharisees. An obvious hindrance Paul faced was the luxury of looking back on his past notoriety and successes. He wrote,

> *"But what things were gain to me, these I have counted loss for Christ. Yet indeed I also count all things loss for the excellence of the knowledge of Christ Jesus my Lord, for whom I have suffered the loss of all things, and count them as rubbish, that I may gain Christ"* (Philippians 3:7-8).

It was as difficult for me to let go of the success in my past as it was my failures. Looking at my past accomplishments released a flood of remorse, self-pity and even self-hatred. I found myself wanting to relive and recreate my past rather than live in and for my future. This time it wasn't a failure that slowed me down, but my cherished and storied memories. One day, God spoke openly to me. Again, while not audible, it was deafening. *"If you don't stop looking back on your success, you will always measure yourself by your past and never come into the new thing I am creating you to be."*

This principle encompasses all of life. We need to release successes just as surely as we release our failures. Stop looking at the glory days and ask the Lord to reveal His new assignment. After all, He is doing a new thing in you.

FAILURE FROM GOD'S ⸜

We will never rebound until we see ou⸜
perspective. Once exiled to Babylon, Israel hardı⸜
former self. Isaiah 42:22 describes Israel's appalling ⸜

> *"This is a people robbed and plundered; all of them
> are snared in holes, and they are hidden in prison
> houses; they are for prey, and no one delivers; for
> plunder, and no one says, 'Restore!'"*

Read these words slowly. *"Robbed—plundered—snared in
holes—in prison—no one delivers—no one says restore."* Reading
God's description of His people is not easy on the ears. They had
fallen so badly no one believed Israel could come back from such
a lowly state. No one said, *"Restore,"* because no one thought
anyone who had fallen so low could return to their former glory.
God's perspective, however, was different. A true prophet not only
diagnoses the disease accurately but sees God's willingness to heal.
Isaiah didn't leave them in a failed past. He continues,

> *"But now, thus says the Lord, who created you, O
> Jacob, and He who formed you, O Israel: 'Fear not,
> for I have redeemed you; I have called you by your
> name; you are Mine. For I am the Lord your God, the
> Holy One of Israel, your Savior.*
>
> *"'Let all the nations be gathered together, and
> let the people be assembled. Who among them can
> declare this, and show us former things? Let them
> bring out their witnesses, that they may be justified;
> or let them hear and say, "It is truth"'* (Isaiah 43:1,9).

Even after repeated failures, God did not write His people off.
Instead, He looked at their repulsive condition and redeemed them.
Like my dad (I mentioned in an earlier chapter) who took joy in
restoring wrecked vehicles, God looks at broken people like us and
says, "I'll take you. Now watch how your shattered life becomes a

witness to My transforming power." And why would God rebound failures such as us? Is it because we suddenly perform better or pray more? No. God simply says, *"You are Mine. I am the Lord your God, the Holy One of Israel, your Savior"* (bold added). There's one reason. We belong to Jesus, and that's enough.

I love two little, often overlooked words in this passage: *"But now."* God says, "That was then; *this is now."* From here forward, everything changes. The crowning moment comes when everyone witnesses the return of what was a hopeless situation and proclaims, *"It is truth!"* It can also be said this way, "Look at what God did!"

You have come to your *"But now"* moment in history. God sees you plundered by guilt, ensnared by depression, imprisoned in shame, with very few, if any, who truly believe you will come back. *"But now"* things will shift. Your fall and failure? That was then. God's perspective is different. His view is always redeeming.

"YOU ARE MINE"

When I was a young boy, a tragedy occurred one night that marked how I would later view God's perspective of me.

I was in the twilight of sleep when flashing lights swirling around the bedroom walls awakened me. My ten-year-old eyes had never seen anything like this in living color. The only thing close was Walter Cronkite's evening news clips of the Vietnam War I'd watched on our nineteen-inch, black-and-white TV set. With heart racing, I hurried to my parents' bedroom to find Mama holding a cup of coffee, looking out the window.

"What happened?" She could feel the fear in my voice.

"Someone wrecked a car in our yard," she answered while her eyes remained riveted to the window. "Now you go back to bed."

Fat chance of that now. In my Roy Rogers PJs I waddled through our little house out the back door to watch from our driveway. Daddy was already outside huddled with other men, closer to the accident than I dared get. The next thing I saw and heard will live inside me forever.

170

Suddenly a car sped to the scene, slammed on brakes and stopped. The car door swung open, and a woman, whom I later discovered was the mother of the victim, ran full gait toward the car resting on its side. Police officers and firefighters grabbed her to keep her at a distance. Yanking her arms to free herself from her protectors, she cried out, "Let me go. He's mine! He's mine! He's mine!"

Later that week, eavesdropping on chats at the community store, I heard the mother's son lay lifeless on the ground beside his car. In a drunken stupor he lost control and hit the power pole. Worse still, the pole penetrated the windshield of his car, decapitating him. Knowing he was to blame, his mother found him not looking human, much less like her son. Even so, to deny him now would be to deny herself. She could not. She did not. "He's mine! He's mine!"

My young mind could not imagine that thirty years later I would lie lifeless beside my own wreckage. Mine, however, was a moral collapse that left me looking nothing like the well-known leader my city once knew. It felt very much the same as when I watched the flashing lights of emergency vehicles in our yard. A few people came near, but most stood at a distance and gawked in disbelief. I lay mangled from bad choices. Our little city had never experienced anything in real life like this before. Neither had I.

Alone one day, with a Bible in my lap and my eyes fixed out my bedroom window, I was a spiritual and emotional basket case. Just then a familiar Presence I missed so badly drew near. He wasn't put off by my lifelessness or losses. I hardly recognized myself, but my Father knew me, and He came near that day. As His Presence wrapped around my wounded soul, I silently worshipped. I was too weak for volume, but within I worshipped Him. As I did, I think I heard Him say, "You're Mine! You're Mine! You're Mine!"

MOVING ON

The phrase "And it came to pass" is recorded in the Bible more than 180 times. It only proves God is more interested in where we're going than where we've been. There comes a time when He wants us to let the past pass.

171

You cannot change the disorder from your history, but you can be reconciled to it, forgiven for it and learn from it as you move into your God-designed future. What happened and what you did are not who you are. Neither is it who you shall be.

Your history stands written, and it is a fact. *"But now,"* God says, *"I have redeemed you; I have called you by your name."* God's *"But now"* changes everything, including the labels that come with a troubled past. In the next chapter, you'll discover God has even changed your name.

Chapter Sixteen

What Is Your Name?

God never defines us by our failures. Instead, He calls us by a name that values us and glorifies Him. Our part is to believe we are who He says we are until that is who we become.

The first word we learn to cherish is our name. Research has discovered that, when we hear our name, multiple regions of the brain are activated. These findings are evidence that hearing our name triggers brain functions that are unique to hearing our own name when compared to hearing someone else's name.[5]

In grade school, hearing the teacher call my name in class made me shiver. I'd draw up and want to hide from her and twenty-five other pairs of beady eyes that were suddenly interested in me. On the other hand, on the playground, when the two best athletes in the class chose teams for a game of kickball, I'd swell with pride when I heard, "I'll take Billy!" It was especially true if I was their first choice.

Your name matters.

Authority to Name

Where does one get the authority to impart something so important like a name? It started in the beginning when God asked

Adam to help Him with the creation process by naming the animal kingdom. Genesis 2:19 says,

> *"Out of the ground the Lord God formed every beast of the field and every bird of the air, and brought them to Adam to see what he would call them. And whatever Adam called each living creature, that was its name."*

The one given authority has the power to name. God bestowed upon Adam authority to give each creature a name, and whatever he called it that was its name. The principle is still active today.

My parents (because they were "my parents") had the legal authority to name me, William Ray Baldwin. On a more trivial note, my sister, nine years my elder, tells how she and Mom squabbled about my name. My sister wanted a little brother named "Billy Ray," but Mom wouldn't allow it. Instead, she named me "William," after my dad. I suppose Mom appeased Sis by using "Ray" as my middle name. Throughout my childhood Sis and my cousins called me "Billy Ray," so Sis got her way after all. Among family members, that name stayed with me until I outgrew it.

Years later, when I played high school football, my teammates nicknamed me "Bubba" because Bubba Smith, the all-pro defensive end for the Baltimore Colts, was my favorite NFL player. Since we played the same position, he was my role model. I dreamed of being as good as Bubba.

I took pride in being called by the name of my favorite player. When I heard my coach scream from the sidelines, "Get 'em, Bubba!" something happened inside me. Hearing that name made me feel like I *was* Bubba Smith.

Here's the critical question. Who gave the authority to change my name?

I did. And I not only allowed it, but I also encouraged it.

The name Bubba stuck much longer than I anticipated. More than thirty years after graduating from high school and moving away, I was driving through my hometown and stopped at a store for gas.

While paying the clerk, I faintly heard, "Hey, Bubba!" but paid no attention. "Bubba!" The second time caught my ear. I turned to find an old high school teammate I had not seen in years. Even after decades, to him I was Bubba.

Names can stick with us, define us and even change us. The names we allow or choose are the names we will be known by and eventually become. Herein lies a principle of life.

> *When we accept a name, we impart the authority and*
> *approval to be conformed to the image and character*
> *it conveys.*

In the New Testament, the word translated as "name" means "character." The name we give ourselves and allow others to call us has the potential to conform us to the character of the name itself. When my teammates called me Bubba, in my imagination it was as if I walked back to the dressing room and returned to the field as another man. A character shift took place, and a different energy and attitude came over me. It was only psychological, but it worked nonetheless.

Adam was given authority to name God's creatures, and *"whatever Adam called each living creature, **that was its name**"* (Genesis 2:19, bold added). Thus each animal *became* the name Adam gave it.

Not every name will push us upward. Some things people call us can send us plummeting to depressing lows. The point is, *we are the deciding factor*. We relinquish authority to names that lift us up or send us spiraling downward.

THE PURPOSE AND DESTINY OF A NAME

In the ancient Eastern world parents named their children for the meaning behind a name. They revealed their hopes and dreams for their child in the name they gave them. They believed a child would grow into the character of their name. So the ancients named their children for purpose and destiny, rather than mere identity.

For example, the book of Genesis tells the story of Jacob, the younger of twin boys, born just seconds after his brother, Esau. As the twins were being born, Esau came first with Jacob literally on his heels. Scripture says, *"His hand took hold of Esau's heel; so his name was called Jacob"* (Genesis 25:26). The children's parents named Esau's twin brother for something he did when he was not even sixty seconds old.

Jacob is a name that has a triple meaning. It means "he who grabs the heel," but it also means "to deceive" and "usurp." Did Isaac and Rebekah name him on a whim because they were amused at the child holding onto the heel of his brother born ahead of him? Surely Jacob's parents knew the full implications of his name, or did they?

As it turned out, Jacob grew up and personified every aspect of his name. Jacob was a determined young man who desired the possessions and position of an elder brother. Taking advantage of his weary and hungry brother, Jacob "tripped up" Esau, convincing him to trade his father's blessing for food (heel grabber). Then Jacob deceived his father, Isaac (deceiver), and swindled him out of the birthright, traditionally reserved for the first-born son (usurper). If the second-born twin got his name for being the cute little "heel-grabber" at birth, it's unlikely his family was as entertained by the grown-up version of Jacob. As he grew into every facet of his name, he caused a rift in the family.

LABELED BY FAILURE

The Gospel of John 8:3-11 tells the story of religious leaders dragging a woman before Jesus. I'm sure she had a name, but we know her and label her by her failure. We call her "the woman caught in adultery."

> *"Then the scribes and Pharisees brought to Him a woman caught in adultery. And when they had set her in the midst, they said to Him, 'Teacher, this woman was caught in adultery, in the very act. Now Moses, in the law, commanded us that such should be stoned. But what do you say?' This they said, testing Him, that they might have something of which*

*to accuse Him. But Jesus stooped down and wrote
on the ground with His finger, as though He did not
hear"* (John 8:3-5).

Scribes and Pharisees accused her, while Jesus, appearing
uninterested in what they had to say, stooped down stirring in the
dirt. With their eyewitnesses and scriptural proof-texts, the scribes
and Pharisees sneered over their right to stone her. And yet it wasn't
the woman they were after at all. They wanted Jesus. His popularity
provoked their jealousy, and they considered Him far too lenient on
people like her. So they set Him up by bringing a woman caught in
the act of sexual scandal. Armed with the law of Moses, on the one
hand, and sinful evidence, on the other, they aimed to back Him into
a corner. They planned to force Him to side with either the Jews or
the adulteress.

Imagine with me the scene. Jesus looks at the woman's shamed,
tear-stained face then glances up at the scowling eyes of her accusers
and back down at the ground. He breaks His silence.

"Okay. You've made your point. Stone her. *But. . .*"

He pauses.

"The one among you who has *never sinned. . .*"

Jesus tilts His head upward. His eyes meet theirs before He
continues.

"In any way. . ."

Beads of sweat begin to pop up on the brows of the men with
rocks in their hands.

"*You* throw the first stone."

The silence was uncomfortably loud.

Jesus does not look back up. Crouched beside the barely covered
woman on one side, with the religious leaders standing on the other,
He continues doodling in the dirt.

The next sounds were the "thud" of rocks, one by one, dropping
to the ground. The hands of the woman's accusers grew limp, and
the stones slipped from their fingertips. Beginning with the oldest,
the hagglers moped away without a peep.

Jesus stops whisking the dust, and I visualize Him now writing
legibly. What He wrote is speculation. No one knows. But we all

like to think we do. I have my ideas. Writing where the woman could see, I want to believe He etched out the word "Tetelestai." It means *it's over—paid in full.*

It's a legal term used in the courts of that day. After a prisoner served his full prison sentence, they gave him a legal document with the word *Tetelestai* stamped with Rome's seal. It served as official notice that the criminal had been legally released from prison. It's also the last word Jesus spoke while dying on the cross. *"It is finished"* (John 19:30). *Tetelestai.* It's over. You, too, have been legally released from your prison of guilt and shame.

"Where are those accusers of yours? Has no one condemned you?" Jesus asked in John 8:10. He wanted the woman to hear herself say it.

"No one, Lord" (John 8:11).

She was fascinated at how the kindness of Jesus diffused the disgust of the religious men. Grace does this. Grace is to accusation and condemnation what water is to a fire.

Half dressed, nothing but a blanket partly covering her, the woman caught in adultery is no longer embarrassed. She looks into the eyes of Jesus and sees an ocean of love so wide she could swim a lifetime and never reach the shore.

"Neither do I condemn you; go and sin no more" (John 8:11).

Both the religious leaders and the woman discovered something that day. In our heart of hearts, we're not always what people perceive us to be. God knows who we genuinely are. And yet He will lovingly exchange the name *Adulterer* with *Pure*, and *Prideful* with *Humbled*. Names and labels disappear when we stand in His presence. *"You shall be called by a new name, which the mouth of the Lord will name"* (Isaiah 62:2).

CHOOSING A NAME

Proverbs 22:1 makes an interesting statement about a name. *"A good name is to be chosen rather than great riches, loving favor rather than silver and gold."* Read the first part of the verse again, slowly this time. *"A good name"* — don't miss the next four words — *"is to be chosen."*

We assume names are given to us, not chosen. Intentional or not, day-to-day living can be helped or hindered by the names and labels people give us. My high school teammates intentionally called me Bubba, and I delightfully received it. In that context the name brought honor. But I've also been tagged with names like Fallen, Liar, Divorcee and Failure, just to mention a few. We cannot control people's opinions, but we can restrict the authority their views have to define who we are.

You have the right to reject names that don't fit the destiny God gives you. We get labeled for our failures, physical makeup, race and countless other silly things. Though they may accurately describe your current condition, if they don't fit your future purpose, let them go. Like Eastern parents in the days of old, God names us for purpose and destiny, not from our past or current identity.

The labels people give, indeed, may contain a measure of truth. The woman mentioned in the eighth chapter of John was known as "the woman caught in adultery" because the name matched her circumstances. The accusation was a fact. Jesus, however, paid no attention to the label. He saw her destiny which looked nothing like the shamed woman they threw before Him.

It's not that her actions didn't matter. They did. But from my take on the story Jesus takes the focus off her adultery to focus on her destiny. He does not condone her affair, but neither does He magnify it. Jesus calls out her God-given destiny by inviting her to receive His unconditional love and a new beginning into a life of purity. What's more, He does this before she could prove herself worthy to be called by a name other than "the woman caught in adultery." Jesus renamed her, so to speak, before her present had any resemblance to her future. *He calls us by what we shall be, rather than labeling us for what we appear to be.*

179

If you listen with your heart, you will hear God whispering your name. It's likely to be a dream of who you always wanted to be and something you've always wanted to do. Did you think it was only your wild imagination? Nope. It was God. If the name sounds too good to be true, chances are it's Him. So, from this point forward, you will be choosing a good name.

Change Your Name and Change Your Destiny

At one of Israel's worst times in history, Isaiah prophesies a bleak outlook for their future. His cutting words mark how far they've fallen. In Isaiah 59:2 the prophet declares, *"Your iniquities have separated you from your God; and your sins have hidden His face from you, so that He will not hear."* Even so, their failures would not keep God from giving His people another chance to turn from sin and embrace their real purpose. How did God initiate the change? He changed their name.

> *"You shall no longer be termed Forsaken, nor shall your land any more be termed Desolate; but you shall be called Hephzibah, and your land Beulah; for the Lord delights in you, and your land shall be married"* (Isaiah 62:4).

Israel had fallen into such disgrace that other nations called them *"Forsaken"* and *"Desolate."* God, however, changed their name to *"Delight"* (Hephzibah) and *"Married ones"* (Beulah). Isaiah gave this prophecy when Israel had no appearance as a pure, delightful bride. God lovingly removed the names that brought disgrace and gave new names that portrayed who He envisioned them to be.

Consider all the people in Scripture who were renamed long before they held any likeness to their new name. God met Jacob in a wrestling match and changed his name from Jacob—*the deceiver*—to Israel—*God prevails*. God changed Jacob's name before he proved himself worthy to wear it.

Jesus renamed Simon Bar-Jonah, Peter, *the rock*. He gave Simon a new name knowing all along that before the rooster crowed Peter would deny Him three times. But Jesus also knew Peter would grow into his name and become a rock in His kingdom.

The Lord sees you the same way. Even when your track record isn't so delightful, He delights in you. The names and labels of your past (if even factual) are not what God intended for you. You may currently look nothing like the name God confers upon you, but don't allow labels to keep you tethered to a sad past. You either choose God's new name He gives or by default take a lesser one that cannot fulfill His good purpose and destiny. *A good name is to be chosen.*

Receiving Your New Name

You will need to consider three things as you prepare to welcome the name God gives you. There are no shortcuts.

First, give God the authority to reveal His purpose and plan to you. It's true that the Lord already has all authority, and we really can't give Him any more than He already has. I have found, however, that He does not always exercise this power against our will. If we want to choose our path, we can. We do have a choice as to whom we will follow and believe.

The name He gives may look nothing like what you would choose for yourself. His purpose may feel too big and above your pay grade. Or it may appear smaller than you thought it would be. The destiny is hidden within the name and is always a perfect match for you. God uniquely created you for the task whether big or small. Even tedious assignments become fulfilling experiences when received as the assignment from God. Release the hold others have placed on you, and say yes to what He says about you.

Second, we receive the new name by faith. People with less-than-the-best histories find it difficult to call themselves by names that reflect anything other than what they think they deserve. Likewise, a self-confident person may be offended by a name that suggests a lesser role. In either case, faith comes alive when we accept God's destiny with humility.

God changed Abram's name (exalted father) to Abraham (father of a multitude) when he was ninety-nine years old, and his wife was ninety. They were childless and past childbearing age. Even so, God said, *"I have made you a father of many nations"* (Genesis 17:5). It takes faith and courage to receive a name that could make you look ridiculous before people.

God gave Abram a name that matched his fruitful future, rather than his barren past. I'm sure at times he thought, "Maybe God didn't speak to me, after all. Perhaps the name Abraham is a bit of a stretch. We don't have one child, and yet I'm calling myself a father of nations?" It was up to Abram to choose God's name or continue as usual. *To choose God's fruitful purpose over his barren past, Abram would have to accept by faith his new name, for only an Abraham could become a father of nations.* And so it is with you.

The third part of the process is possibly the most vital. Throughout Scripture God revealed names and destinies to those who were alone. Perhaps it was the absence of distractions that positioned them to hear more clearly. It's no coincidence that during seasons of loneliness, quietness and even distress God revealed His purpose. Learn to be alone with God and cherish it.

Abram was alone when God called him to leave Ur and launch out on a journey of faith. Abram was alone when God changed his name from Abram to Abraham.

Jacob was alone when he wrestled with the man, who turned out to be the God who changed his name to Israel.

Saul of Tarsus, the zealous and intelligent young Pharisee, was larger than life among his peers. On a mission to Damascus to persecute Christians, Jesus sovereignly revealed Himself to Saul. He was thrown from his horse, blinded and arose talking to Jesus.

We don't know when or how it happened, but Saul of Tarsus became Paul, an apostle of Jesus Christ. Saul means "asked for," and surely the Jews admired and "asked for" the fervent and brilliant Saul of Tarsus. Paul means "little one," which could mean that God gave him a name that kept him small in the eyes of men.

Paul spent much of his life instructing the churches he established through letters he wrote from jail. Those letters became more than half of the New Testament. He did this, mind you, while alone. The name *Paul* was a play on words, for he was anything but small in the eyes of God.

Handle your new name with wisdom. Abram never publicly called himself *Abraham*, and Paul never introduced himself using the title "*apostle* Paul." Who you are and who you are becoming will be revealed as you surrender your life to God. Names are not always meant to be used. Sometimes they are simply *lived*.

GOD IS NOT ASHAMED OF YOU

God is not ashamed to be identified with your past. Why? His destiny always celebrates the redemption of our failed history. For people who want to keep you in their category of being a loser, you could do precious little to satisfy their legal demands. In humility turn your attention to God's plan for you.

One last time let's revisit Jacob. At birth his name shaped his destiny, and his life became a drama filled with devious motives.

The first time anyone questioned Jacob's identity, it was his father, Isaac, who asked, *"Who are you, my son?"* (Genesis 27:18). Jacob had always wanted to be someone he was not. He did not want to be the second-born, heel-grabbing twin, so he lied to his father. *"I am Esau your first born"* (Genesis 27:19). Notice that Jacob made sure to add *"your first born."* What he lusted for was Esau's position. Jacob had always wanted to be *first*, something he could not change. To get what he wanted, he lied.

The second time we see someone asking Jacob his name was when he wrestled with *"the Man,"* who was none other than God Himself (see Genesis 32:24). God asked him, *"What is your name?"* (Genesis 32:27). This time around, Jacob didn't lie or hide his true identity as he did with his father, Isaac. After all, God knew Jacob to the core, just as He knows you and me. *"He said, 'Jacob'"* (Genesis 32:27). He readily admits to God, "I am a deceiver."

183

Jacob walked away from that confrontation with a limp that remained with him the rest of his life. His limp would forever mark his encounter with God. And yet Jacob hobbled away bearing a new name. *"Your name shall no longer be called Jacob, but Israel; for you have struggled with God and with men, and have prevailed"* (Genesis 32:28). The mystery of a genuine encounter with God is it leaves us weaker but strengthened—stumbling and yet soaring like an eagle.

God is a good Father who will not shame us for our past but re-identifies us to walk into our future, though we do so with a limp. When Jacob humbled himself, God exalted him. Humility remains God's method whereby He bestows upon us a new name. *"Therefore humble yourselves under the mighty hand of God, that He may exalt you in due time"* (1 Peter 5:6). From Jacob's new name, *Israel*, a nation was born.

I am encouraged that in the Bible it's the old name Jacob, not Israel, most often used when identifying him with God. *"God remembered His covenant with Abraham, with Isaac, and **with Jacob**"* (Exodus 2:24, bold added). Even through all of Jacob's shenanigans, God was not ashamed to be called the "God of Jacob."

He is not ashamed of you either. The new name He gives you may portray new roles, relationships or dreams. Do not fear to confess who He says you are becoming. And then don't hold back identifying with the new name God gives you. It's not a matter of deserving it, for you could never earn His gifts. The question is, will you receive it?

WHAT IS YOUR NAME?

It is grace that brings us from the pigpen of failure to the front porch of the Father. And wonder of wonders, as we mount the steps and peer into the front door, we discover a party brewing inside. To our amazement, the festivity is in our honor. The only things the Father demands we leave outside are the names and labels of our past.

"I am no longer worthy to be called your son. Make me like one of your hired servants" (Luke 15:19).

He will interrupt us before we call ourselves by anything less than the family name. We deserve to be a *"hired servant."* After all, we still reek of the stench of our failure. But, behold, you are still His son, His daughter, and He will not deny His own. *"My son was dead and is alive again"* (Luke 15:24). Who are we to call ourselves by a name that's less honoring than the one He gives us?

What is your name? I'm not referring to the name on your birth certificate or the one you think you deserve now that life has gone sour. Pull away. Get alone with Him and listen because He's calling your name. His name is always good and promising and hopeful.

Chapter Seventeen

The Promise

I am grateful to have lived long enough to know falling and rising, failure and recovery. I've discovered that both are gifts of God's mercy.

Over the last twenty years my wife and I have moved four times. Without fail, in every home a drawer in our kitchen becomes our junk drawer. It's always the kitchen and always near a door entering the kitchen from outside. I say it *becomes* our junk drawer because neither of us discusses a plan to designate such a space; it just happens.

Our junk drawer is a litter bin of has-beens, with nothing in it having any likeness or connection to anything else. It's where we stuff our too-valuable-to-throw-away-but-should-not-be-seen junk—the kind of junk you don't want to leave lying around in plain sight.

I thought we were a minority. I wondered, do other families have similar dysfunctional spaces? In an internet search I typed in "Junk Drawer" and was dumbfounded at the gazillion links that emerged. Junk drawers, it seems, are standard in homes. I found websites to help you organize your junk drawer, and you can even purchase junk drawer starter kits. Like parts of our anatomy, just about everyone has one, and for a good reason.

Junk drawers help us look neat and tidy. We always position ours in a convenient place where if an unexpected visitor shows up we can cram our clutter into it. With a pull and a swipe our kitchen can look shipshape in thirty seconds, and we appear more junk free than we are. We don't mind admitting we have our junk, but we would rather people not see it.

Such is the life of people who know the pain of a blundering failure. We tend to create a mental storage vat, a junk drawer where we stuff the images of yesterday's failures. For years I packed my junk inside a fake smile and cheery voice. When church folk were near, *especially* church folk, I tried my darnedest to shove my past into my mental garbage disposal to appear more together than I was. After all, I reasoned, people don't expect good people, especially "pastor types" to have garbage. Right? Well, consider this.

Jesus has already provided forgiveness for sins—junk—you have yet to commit. That's right—I said, "Yet to commit." That means nothing you did, do or will do takes Him by surprise. He saw it coming. Trying to wrap your head around this thought can give you a theological migraine, but it's true. Jesus' sacrifice on the cross saves us from sin, past, present and future. His mercy is for sinning sinners *and* sinning saints. As I pointed out in chapter 2, most of the Bible is about God chasing down *His people,* not to slam us, but to save us. If you trace humanity all the way back to Adam, we're *all* His people.

The transformation that restores us to God and His purposes is a process, rather than a single event. Perhaps the first light that shines into our darkness is so much higher than anything we've experienced before, we feel wholly transformed after our first encounter with God's love. But we soon find change of the total person takes time. The Bible says it's a *"race set before us"* (see Hebrews 12:2). We discover this race is not a sprint but a marathon. We, the runners, live it out on a track we call "life." We're in this for the long haul, for transformation comes over time.

If Scripture and experience have taught me anything, I've learned saints are not always saintly, and good people are not always good. We don't always run well. We trip and fall, skin our knees, bruise our souls, bleed profusely and look a mess. We take wrong exits and lose our way and make bad decisions and gorge ourselves on things we thought we had lost an appetite for. We find we are as much in need of grace *now* as we were the first time we took the hand of Jesus to follow Him. We are discovering Christ died not only for sinners far from God, but also for the failed and fallen seasoned saint. His mercy, the same mercy we received when we first met Him, remains there for us when we've fallen face down. *His love never leaves. Never.*

The apostle Paul said we are *"transformed by the renewing of our mind"* (Romans 12:2). Our mind is the location of the junk drawer of our failures. Our mind is where we stuff the people, pain and past—all the debris connected to our blunders. We cram memories from failure into a mental junk bin because they're just too painful to look at, and we don't want anyone else knowing about them either. Refuse from our past smolders on the junk heap of our failed history.

So, along come our accuser and accusers, to point the finger of accusation, reminding God and us of blunders and broken promises we did not keep. And it's here, standing on the rim of our contaminated waste dump that we must courageously declare the word of the Lord over our lives. It helps to have a friend who believes in the God who rebounds to proclaim His Word to us. But if there's no one else we have His Word and His Spirit living within us to make this declaration ourselves. And, of course, through the book you hold in your hands, you have me.

I WILL RESTORE

One cannot read the wavering history of God's people without being astounded with His persistence to rebound us from our many falls. Like the Old Testament prophets I recalled in earlier chapters, Joel reminded Israel they were on the verge of reaping a harvest from their disobedience. They were already experiencing crop failures and economic catastrophes. Israel's junk drawer was spilling over with yesterday's defiance. The fruit of their foolishness brought such despair upon them that Joel described it as *"a day of darkness and gloominess"* (Joel 2:2). Many of us have experienced such a day. Even so, the Rebounder Himself could not restrain Himself from declaring the impossible and unimaginable. He did not give up on His people (He never does) but boldly proclaimed to restore them to their former glory and destiny.

> *"So **I will restore** to you the years that the swarming locust has eaten. . .You shall eat in plenty and be satisfied, and praise the name of the Lord your God, who has dealt wondrously with you; and My people shall never be put to shame"* (Joel 2:25-26, bold added).

I've already pointed out that God will not protect us from all the consequences of our choices. And yet even the fallout of failure would not prevail over the One who grabs the rebound and wins the game. He proclaimed He would restore, and He did so in an era when it was theologically and humanly unheard of. No human being can turn back the hands of time and recover what they tossed to the wind. God, however, can restore years eaten up by the grim circumstances of failure. God's rebound is so overwhelmingly complete that the praises of the restored will catch the attention of the world and cause them to marvel at God's grace and goodness.

I will restore.

Our junk drawers that once concealed memories of shame will transform into a showcase displaying trophies of praise. The facts of our failures will no longer hold us captive, for shame cannot settle in the heart of the restored. Shame is swallowed up in the wondrous mercy of a God who restores us to Himself and to His destiny in our lives. We discover Jesus truly is greater than our junk.

I will restore.

These words are God's promise to us. God gave this promise at a time when Jewish people related to Him through *dos* and *don'ts*. Their staggering and stumbling, however, would not silence His desire to have a people on the earth that would testify of His greatness, goodness and grace. Something bigger was at stake than broken rules, and that was God's broken heart.

A prophecy from a man we call a minor prophet created a major upheaval on the earth and in the heavens. Joel enters the scene to reveal the heartbeat of love from a God who restores. He declared this promise before these people showed signs of repentance. Was a turn-around necessary? Unquestionably, yes. But now they would not only repent *of* sin but *unto* a promise.

I will restore.

This promise reverberated throughout the galaxies under an old covenant far more inferior to the *"better covenant"* (Hebrews 8:6) we are privileged to have today. If God was eager to fulfill His promise then, how much more is He willing to do so now? It's impossible for God to decree a thing and not perform it. Do we have responsibilities to walk out? Certainly. But when He desires it, it's as good as done. He watches over His word to perform it (Jeremiah 1:12).

I will restore.

Who says you can't start over again? Perhaps you've already tried to get up so many times that your "new beginnings" have become "old hat."

"What's the use?" you ask. "People will only mock when I tell them I'm trusting God to help me this time."

Read the account of the prophet Elijah's drought-breaking prayer for rain (1 Kings 18:41-48). He prayed seven times before he saw any evidence of rain on the horizon. And even then the cloud that appeared was only the size of a man's hand. But it was a beginning, and fortunately Elijah knew rebounding from a three-and-a-half-year drought would be a process. Even a small cloud can become a toad-strangling downpour!

Think about how even Jesus had to pray twice for a blind man to receive clear vision (Mark 8:22-26). After His first prayer the man's sight returned and yet was blurry. But Jesus stayed at it until He received the twenty-twenty result He knew was possible.

Do you think your junk drawer is too full for God's promise?

Who are you to say, "I've tried before, but failed?"

If this is your response, I want to remind you of a promise. These are not words from an author or a preacher. These words come from God Himself about people like us.

I will restore.

One of my favorite movies is the classic *Chariots of Fire*. It's a true story based on the 1924 summer Olympics. The main character is Eric Liddle. He was a Scotsman ranked as one of the best runners in the world who ran for Scotland's national track team. Liddle is a Christian and plans to enter the ministry after college. At this time in his life, however, he knows he is supposed to run track. He tells his family, "I feel the pleasure of God when I run."

A year before the Olympics, Scotland is in a meet with England and Ireland, and Liddle is in the 440-yard run. After the runners take off, they battle for position to get the inside lane. In the group Eric Liddle gets his feet tangled up with a runner from England and falls. Lying on the ground, he looks up to see the pack twenty yards ahead of him.

Suddenly Liddle's eyes catch a track official who says, "Get up. You can still run!" He gets up, catches the other runners and challenges the leader at the finish line. Approaching the tape, Liddle edges in front and wins the race. It stands as one of the outstanding finishes in the history of track and field. The turning point came when Eric Liddle heard and acted on the words, "Get up. You can still run!"

You do not have to surrender to failure.

Get up. You can still run!

You can begin again and finish your course. I can't predict where you will be at the finish line, but if you don't get up we both know where you will end up. Finishing depends on you taking courage to get up right where you are. This promise is *your* promise. Not because you're good, but because God is. Not because you think you can do it, but because God promised it.

I will restore.

See you at the finish line.

ABOUT THE AUTHOR

W illiam "Bill" Baldwin received his B.A. in Philosophy and Religion, and earned a Masters Degree in theology with doctoral studies from Emory University, Atlanta, Georgia. He has been a church leader for over forty years beginning his ministry at age 21. Baldwin has planted four churches and addressed leader's groups and conferences in the United States and abroad. Currently, he is the senior leader of Harvest Church in Albemarle, North Carolina.

In 2001 he founded Truth to the Nations, a ministry that encouraged local churches and leaders to pursue a greater passion for Christ. Bill's experience makes him a sought-after leader among churches and pastors, locally and internationally. His wealth of teaching and inspiration opens doors for him as a guest speaker in churches and conferences, as well as a mentor to various church leaders. Locally, he helped found and leads an interdenominational pastors and leaders fellowship where leaders from his city and region collaborate, pray and nurture friendship together.

WilliamBaldwin.org

Endnotes

[1] "Tear down this wall!" Wikipedia, The Free Encyclopedia, last modified June 14, 2018, https://en.wikipedia.org/wiki/Tear_down_this_wall!

[2] Robert E. Coleman and David J. Gyertson, *One Divine Moment: The Account of the Asbury Revival of 1970,* (Old Tappan, New Jersey, Fleming H. Revell Company, 1995), 14-16

[3] I wrestled with this state of mind following my failure. Feelings are not always reliable barometers of our circumstances. Though it certainly "felt like" former church members held me in contempt, time revealed this was not always the case. Shame was the real issue.

[4] Brené Brown, "Shame vs. Guilt," Brene Brown, January 13, 2013, www.brenebrown.com. (accessed May 10, 2018).

[5] Carmody, Dennis and Michael Lewis. "Brain Activation When Hearing One's Own and Others' Names," US National Library of Medicine, National Institutes of Health, September 7, 2006, Ncbi.nlh.nih.gov. (accessed November 7, 2017).

CPSIA information can be obtained
at www.ICGtesting.com
Printed in the USA
FFHW02n0315290918
48592711-52547FF